TO CREATE

A DIFFERENT FUTURE

TO CREATE A DIFFERENT FUTURE

religious hope and

technological planning

kenneth vaux, editor

Friendship Press • New York

Library of Congress Cataloging in Publication Data

Houston Conference on Technology and a Human Future,
Houston, Tex., 1972.
To create a different future.
1. Technology and ethics—Addresses, essays, lectures.
I. Vaux, Kenneth, ed. II. Title.
BJ59.H68   170   72-5202
ISBN 0-377-02041-9

contents

FOREWORD

These are times that try men's souls and one of the great questions today is whether men and women and children will be able to talk together and work together and pray together to solve some of the pressing problems that confront us, or whether people, especially religious people, will retire, count themselves out of the struggle, seek individual salvation or individual comfort, while the world goes to pieces.

I believe that if we are to produce order on this planet, save our endangered environment, reconstruct the institutions that were developed when almost all of us lived on the land, and learn to bring the present closer to the Kingdom of God on earth, then congregations of Christians must take a much more lively part in the thinking that will be needed. Christian congregations are united as communities of trust and hope, and themes discussed in a congregational context can reach a new kind of illumination. In the last decade we have seen crusading clergy and crusading young people struggling to arouse the conscience both of the churches and of the communities around them. But in very few cases have the congregations themselves been actively involved in the dialogue. This is what we need, something more than a duet between the shepherd and the wandering sheep, something closer to the *communitas* that has accompanied every significant advance in the history of the Christian church.

The chapters in this book are provocative, and challenging. They do not call for assent—or dissent—but for consideration. If the traditional methods of defending our homes and our country will no longer suffice in a nuclear age when no people can defend their own children unless they defend the children of the enemy also, if we are consuming too much energy and too many irreplaceable raw materials, if we are risking the safety of the whole planet, if the doctrine of more and more production no longer fits a world that is coming to the end of its carrying capacity, if the kinds of schools and marriages within which we have reared our young through the last century no longer give them the background they need for meeting the terrible pressing problems of the modern world—then discussion that is based on the best objective facts available, and informed by a passion for a better world, must take place among those who trust each other because they share a common ethic and a common hope.

Margaret Mead
New York, January 1972

INTRODUCTION

Since man appeared on the earth he has looked into the future with both hope and dread, then proceeded to make things to avert calamity and achieve his desire. He uses fire to guard from the terror of the night and to warm his home and food. In the modern world man's technical activity expresses this duality. He builds the nuclear submarine to defend his coastline and transport his oil. His antibiotics ward off bacterial attack and sustain well-being.

Hope and dread are human perceptions of the future that bear religious meaning. Whether the future is terrifying or benevolent depends upon spiritual outlook. Is death absurd or meaningful? Can a new society be fashioned or not? Will tomorrow be an open possibility or monotonous repetition of today? Each of these questions poses a religious future-view and most often a technological response.

The Houston Conference on Technology and a Human Future sought to place the issues of a technological future in the context of spiritual meaning and ethical value. As sponsors, we invited participation from all disciplines and professions. The universities and professional schools were represented, as was the business and industrial community. A contingent of high school students and teachers gave a youth perspective.

The papers were prepared on areas of science and technology that make profound impact on man's life and his future. Mankind is deeply troubled today at the points of relation to self, to others, to the world and to God. In each dimension of relatedness, technology poses both threat and promise. Jørgen Randers, a physicist and systems analyst from Norway, placed the theme in a global perspective. Before we can work toward some desirable future we must insure that there is a future. We are now caught up in such a furious process of consumption, growth, pollution and degradation of the environment that the future of human life on the earth is gravely threatened. With simple style and grace Randers opened the conference. About midway through the morning a lean, dark figure leaped onto the platform and began a thrilling part of the two-day dialogue. It was Ivan Illich.

In any estimation Illich is one of the most provocative human beings alive. Taking off from Randers's models of the elements that constitute the good life, Illich began to unfold his vivid critique of our over-structured, over-institutionalized, under-humanized world. The devastating indictment Illich brings is born in his hope for the simple goodness that life could be. The engaging wit and intensity of his manner will long be remembered by the conferees. In his paper written for the symposium he uses the term "conviviality." This is the face-to-face openness to other life on earth, often demeaned by misuse of technology, but a prerequisite as critical to a future quality of life as any technological possibility.

Robert Murray and Robert Francoeur, two scientists concerned with technical alteration of human life at the genetic, embryological and prenatal levels, provided stimulating discussion. Perhaps the greatest challenges that man will face in the near future will be those where technology is applied to human generativity and sexuality.

My paper attempts to weave the insights of the other speakers into a religious and ethical fabric. A spiritual vision of life and the future creates both discontent and hope in a man. He chafes and struggles under the terrible reality of what *is* because he knows what *might* be. A spiritual vision alone can create the models of desirable life and sustain the common will in that pursuit. A vibrant vision of that new world and new humanity promised by God can perhaps best indicate the proximate simulation we should attempt here and now. This essay seeks to find hope symbols that can convey those commitments.

The paper by Robert Murray is based on work originally presented to the Fogarty International Center of the National Institutes of Health in October of 1971. A similar essay along with other reflection on the issues of Genetic Ethics and Counseling will soon be published by a university press for the Institute of Society, Ethics and the Life Sciences. Randers' essay will be published in altered form by The Systems Dynamics Group at M.I.T. We appreciate the chance to include these essays in the context of this symposium.

The Conference was part of the ongoing efforts of the Institute of Religion and Human Development to raise the crucial questions of meaning and value in the scientific center of Houston. The concluding commentary by Drs. Ashley, Hemphill, Lipscomb, Moraczewski and Taggart offer our faculties' multidisciplinary response and analysis. The reflections of a political scientist-philosopher, medical student, physician-internist, psychopharmacologist and psychologist in turn place the issues in broad cultural perspective. These men represent the scientific, clinical and pastoral commitments of the Institute. Their reflections attempt to relate these urgent issues to ethically concerned people in the parishes and synagogues of our country in their efforts to meet these challenges.

The inspiration for the conference came from the editor's participation on The Task Force on the Future of Mankind and the Role of the Christian Churches in a World of Science-Based Technology, a joint venture of the National Council of Churches and Union Theological Seminary. The leadership of co-chairmen Margaret Mead and Roger Shinn and executive director J. Edward Carothers in the international and American work on these problems and the preparation of this volume is greatly appreciated. As Randers suggests, the time horizon and sustaining energy to resolve these problems and create a good future are only possible if the faith communities and congregations of this land and all lands find a new hope and compassion. This volume is dedicated to the churches in their ongoing quest for that future.

The Conference was ably directed by Bert Anson, a life scientist presently working as research associate in our Institute's programs in medical education. Jean Tennant and Marilynn Nixon helped administer the meeting and prepare the manuscript.

The Zale Foundation and the Texas Medical Center institutions offered appreciated support to the Conference. The committee who thoughtfully advised and planned the meeting included: Miguel F. da Cunha, Ph.D., Institute of Religion and Human Development; Ron Durham, Rice University; Janice Harris, Baylor College of Medicine; Mike Hemphill, Baylor College of Medicine; Carol Kelleher, St. Rose Parish; Scott Kelso, Kelso and McCollum, Inc.; Harry Lipscomb, M.D., Baylor College of Medicine; John Mauldin, Rice University; Gwenn Pierre, Texas Southern University; Harold Rorschach, Ph.D., Rice University; Kelton Rotrock, University of Texas School of Public Health; Virginia Sicola, Texas Women's University; Philip Snider, Ph.D., University of Houston; Elneita Stewart, Ed.D., Texas Southern University; Don Williamson, Ph.D., Institute of Religion and Human Development.

Kenneth Vaux
Houston, Texas
February, 1972

GLOBAL LIMITATIONS AND HUMAN RESPONSIBILITY

jørgen randers

JØRGEN RANDERS

Most people today see that our world is joyously riding some uncontrolled roller coaster to impending catastrophe. We know it has to do with population. We know it has to do with ravenous consumption of goods, energy and resources. We know it has to do with our frantic effort to make the earth a great garbage dump and cesspool. The story of how these trends are converging in our world is vividly depicted by Jørgen Randers. The earth lies in the care of all men as do the sky and water. The solidarity and interdependence of global humanity demands that we make immediate common cause in a great effort of repentance, rededication and restoration. Unless we do, the planet will be uninhabitable for our children and we will have betrayed the Maker of all. The following essay reflects the ongoing work of global dynamics carried on by the Systems Dynamics Group at Massachusetts Institute of Technology. Dr. Randers has graciously allowed early publication of this material for which he holds copyright.

> For which of you, desiring to build a tower, does not first sit down and count the cost, whether he has enough to complete it?
>
> Luke 14:28

INTRODUCTION

The main thesis of my essay is very simple: because our environment—the earth—is finite, physical growth cannot continue indefinitely. In spite of its simplicity, the consequences of this fact pose an unprecedented challenge to mankind. The challenge lies in deciding on the ethical basis for making the trade-offs that will confront us in the near future—trade-offs which arise because our globe is finite.

It should be quite unnecessary to point out that our environment is finite. However, most considerations of our future options lose sight of this fact. Thus, it will be worthwhile to spend some time discussing the physical limitations of the earth—especially because it is not generally recognized that we are already quite close to several of the physical limitations that define the carrying capacity of our globe.

AGRICULTURAL LAND

The quantity that is most obviously finite on our earth is our completely inelastic supply of land. There are about 3.2 billion hectares (1 hectare equals approximately 2.47 acres) of land suitable for agriculture on the earth. Approximately half of that land is under cultivation today. The remaining half will require immense capital costs to settle, clear, irrigate or fertilize before it can produce food. The costs will be so high that the United Nations' F.A.O., which is seeking desperately to stimulate greater food production, has decided that in order to expand food output it must rely on more intensive use of currently cultivated land, not on new land development.

If we do decide to incur the costs and to cultivate all possible arable land and to produce as much food as possible, how many people could we expect to feed? The lower curve in Figure 1 shows the amount of land *needed* to feed the growing world population, assuming that the present average of 0.4 hectares per person is sufficient. (If we wanted to feed all of our 3.6 billion people at United States standards, we would require 0.9 hectares per person.) The actual growth in population from 1650 to 1970 is depicted with a heavy line; the projected growth at 2.1 percent per year after 1970 by a

Figure 1 ARABLE LAND

billion hectares

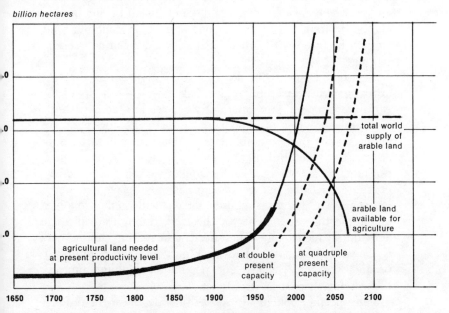

Total world supply of arable land is about 3.2 billion hectares. About 0.4 hectares per person of arable land are needed at present productivity. The curve of land needed thus reflects the population growth curve. The light line after 1970 shows the projected need for land, assuming that world population continues to grow at its present rate. Arable land available decreases because arable land is removed for urban-industrial use as population grows. The dotted curves show land needed if present productivity is doubled or quadrupled.

lighter line. The upper curve indicates the actual amount of arable land available. This line slopes downward because each additional person requires a certain amount of land (0.08 hectares assumed here) for housing, roads, waste disposal, power lines and other uses that essentially "pave" land and make it unusable for farming.

The graph in Figure 1 tells us that, even with the optimistic assumption that we will utilize all possible land, we will still face a desperate land shortage before the year 2000.

The graph also illustrates some very important facts about exponential growth within a limited space. First, it shows how one can move within a few years from a situation of great abundance to one of great scarcity. The human race has had an overwhelming excess of arable land for all of our history, and now within forty years, or one population doubling time, we will be forced to learn to deal with a sudden and serious shortage.

A second lesson to be learned from Figure 1 is that the exact numerical assumptions we make about the limits of the earth are essentially unimportant when we are faced with the inexorable progress of exponential growth. For example, we might assume that *no* arable land is taken for cities, roads, or other non-agricultural uses. In that case, the land available is constant, as shown by the horizontal dashed line, and the point at which the two curves cross is only delayed by about ten years. Or we can suppose that we will double, or even quadruple the productivity of the land, through advances in agricultural technology. The effect of increasing productivity is shown by the dotted lines in Figure 1. Each doubling of productivity gains us just one population doubling time, or thirty to forty years.

Some people look to the sea to provide the extra requirements. But the total world fish catch in 1969 represented only a small percentage of the world's protein, and the total catch in 1970 decreased from 1969. That was the first decrease since the end of World War II. Most experts agree that the world's fish banks have been overfished and that prospects are for further decline, not advances, in protein output. The seas thus cannot eliminate the constraints imposed on growth by limited land.

HEAT RELEASE

We are faced with further obvious constraints in connection with natural resources like fresh water, metals and fuels. Indications are that several of these will be in short supply even at higher prices within the next forty years, if present growth continues. It is argued that mining low grade ores and desalting the sea's water can alleviate these problems, and it may indeed be so, assuming that we can satisfy the concurrent enormous demands for energy.

A consideration of the energy that will be necessary to meet man's growing needs leads us to a more subtle and much more fundamental physical limitation imposed by our environment. Even if we assume that we find the means to *generate* the energy needed—for instance, controlled fusion—we are still faced with the fundamental thermodynamic fact that all energy generated finally ends up as heat. An everyday example is the energy originally stored in the gasoline in your car. A significant part of this energy is immediately released as heat as it warms the engine and the radiator, because the engine is necessarily inefficient in converting the energy in the gasoline to useful torque on the wheels. But the point is that even the *useful* part of the energy finally is transferred to heat in the tires, the road, the brakes and ultimately in the surrounding air. On a larger scale we have the heat release from the cooling of distilled water in a desalination plant.

This final fate of the energy expended should *not* be confused with what is *commonly* called "thermal pollution," namely the waste heat produced locally at the power plant in the generation of electric energy due to inevitable inefficiencies in the generating process. This "thermal pollution" of course also heats the environment, but the point I am making is that even the useful energy output from the plant finally ends up as heat when the energy is used. This is so, irrespective of whether the energy was generated by burning of coal or oil, or by nuclear reactions—and irrespective of what the energy is being used for. It is theoretically impossible to avoid this release if we want to consume energy; no technical gadgetry or scientific breakthrough will circumvent it.

The crucial point is that this heat will begin to have worldwide climatic effects when the released amount reaches some appreciable fraction of the energy normally absorbed from the sun. Thus, if we want to avoid major changes in the climate, there is a fundamental limit to the amount of energy we can consume on earth.

If energy consumption increases at 4 percent a year for another 130 years, we will at that point in time be releasing heat amounting to 1 percent of the incoming solar radiation— enough to increase the temperature of the atmosphere by an estimated 3/4° centigrade. That may sound like an unim-

Figure 2 WASTE HEAT GENERATION IN THE LOS ANGELES BASIN

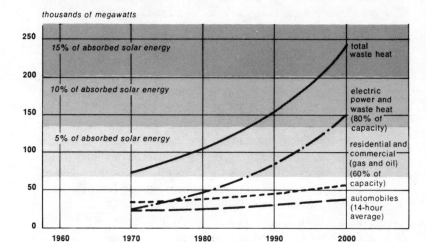

thousands of megawatts

Waste heat released over the 4,000 square mile area of the Los Angeles basin currently amounts to about 5 percent of the total solar energy absorbed at the ground. At the present rate of growth, thermal release will reach 18 percent of incoming solar energy by the year 2000. This heat, the result of all energy generation and consumption processes, is already affecting the local climate.

SOURCE: L. Lees in *Man's Impact on the Global Environment*, Report of the Study of Critical Environmental Problems (Cambridge, Mass.: MIT Press, 1970).

pressive figure, but on a worldwide basis it could amount to climatic upheavals like increased melting of the polar ice caps. Local perturbations may come much sooner. In just thirty years it is estimated that the Los Angeles Basin area will be releasing through its energy consumption 18 percent of the normal incident solar energy of that area (Figure 2).

POLLUTION ABSORPTION

The third limitation I would like to mention is our globe's finite absorptive capacity for pollution. Until quite recently our environment was considered infinite. It seemed incredible that the use of soap for one's laundry and pesticides for one's roses could possibly be able to affect the workings of the world ecosystem. But after the death of Lake Erie, the global increase in atmospheric carbon dioxide and the prohibition in the United States of swordfish due to its content of mercury, it is abundantly clear that our environment is only able to absorb and degrade a limited amount of emissions and waste every year. When we exceed this absorptive capacity, we not only cause pollutants to accumulate in nature, but we also run the risk of completely destroying the natural degradation processes themselves, and decreasing the future absorptive capacity. This general principle can be described in more practical terms: discharging a little bit of waste into a pond will only slightly lower the water quality because the microorganisms manage to degrade the pollution as it occurs. A higher, constant discharge rate will result in a lower but constant water quality. The absorptive capacity of the pond is exceeded, however, if we increase the discharge rate to the point where the lake dies and becomes unable to clear itself. When that happens continued discharge to the pond will simply accumulate, making the water quality continually worse.

Thus we realize that absorptive capacity—far from being a commodity in unlimited supply—is an extremely valuable, scarce resource, that in fact limits the total possible emissions from human activity if we do not want to destroy our life support system.

GROWTH IN A FINITE WORLD

Having now established the existence of purely physical limitations of our earth (and I have described only a few of the many biological, physical and social limits that exist), we may ask whether mankind's present behavior takes into account their existence.

On a global scale we are presently experiencing an exponential growth in population and in what I will call capital— buildings, roads, trucks, power plants, machinery, ships and so on. Some inevitable consequences of this growth are exponentially increasing demands for food and energy and also exponentially increasing emissions of pollution to the environment.

Since we know that there exist upper limits to the supply of food and energy and also to the amount of pollution that can be absorbed by the environment, it seems obvious that the growth we are presently experiencing cannot continue indefinitely. More important, we will surpass several constraints within the next couple of generations.

Hence, we are led to ask: are there mechanisms in the world system as it is currently organized that will cause a smooth shift from present growth trends to some other kind of acceptable behavior consistent with the world's finite capabilities? Or are we heading for some sort of disaster?

These are the questions our group at Massachusetts Institute of Technology set out to answer when we embarked on an effort to make a mathematical simulation model of population and capital growth in the world system.

THE WORLD MODEL

Our model is a set of assumptions that relate world population, industry, pollution, agriculture and natural resources. The model explicitly represents the growth forces as a function of the biological, political, economic, physical and social factors that influence them. Let me give you a brief description of the main ideas underlying our model, and therefore, the world system.

Figure 3

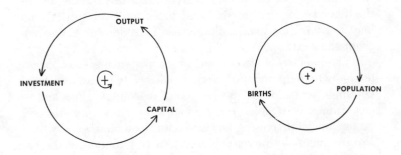

The positive feedback loops governing the growth in population and capital.

The exponential growth of population and capital is an important cause of all global problems—unemployment, starvation, disease, pollution, the threat of warfare and resource shortages. All are influenced importantly by the interaction of population and capital. No attempt to understand our long-term options can succeed unless it is firmly based on an understanding of the relationships between these two forces and of the ultimate limits to their growth.

Population and birth constitute a positive feedback loop (Figure 3). More people produce more births and more births result in more people. Wherever there is a dominant positive feedback loop of this form, exponential growth will be observed. Capital and investment constitute another positive feedback loop. Capital produces output of goods. Greater output, all else equal, results in a larger investment and thus in more capital. The interactions among population and capital determine the rate at which each of them grows. The interaction takes many forms (Figure 4).

As a greater fraction of output is diverted from investment, the growth rate of capital decreases. Output may be diverted to consumption, to services or to agricultural capital such as fertilizer, tractors or irrigation ditches. As services increase, health and education improve, average lifetime becomes greater, deaths decrease and population grows. Similarly, output diverted into agricultural capital results ultimately in more food and a higher average lifetime. The primary determinant of the fraction of output reinvested is the output per capita. Where production per capita is low, most of the output must be diverted to consumption, services and food. Those allocations reduce the rate of accumulation of the capital base and, at the same time, stimulate the growth of population. Population can increase much more easily than capital in traditional societies. Hence, output per capita remains low in these countries and they find it very difficult to achieve economic growth.

Output diverted into consumption subtracts capital from the system and does not directly generate future growth. Industrial output also leads to the depletion of natural resources. As natural resources decline, lower grade ores must be mined and raw material must be transported longer distances. Since more

Figure 4

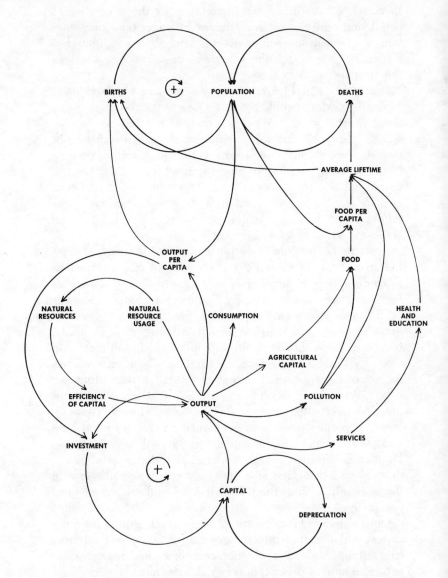

Basic interactions between population growth and capital accumulation.

Figure 5 BIRTH RATES AND GNP PER CAPITA

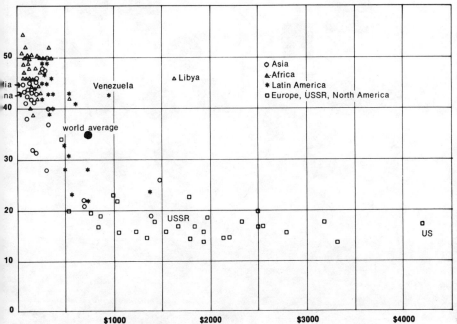

births per thousand people per year

GNP per capita (US dollars per person per year)

Birth rates in the world's nations show a regular downward trend as GNP
per capita increases. More than one-half of the world's people are represented in the upper left-hand corner of the graph, where GNP per capita
is less than $500 per person per year and birth rates range from 40 to 50
per thousand persons per year. The two major exceptions to the trend,
Venezuela and Libya, are oil-exporting nations, where the rise in income
is quite recent and income distribution is highly unequal.

SOURCE: US Agency for International Development, *Population Program Assistance*
(Washington, DC: Government Printing Office, 1970).

capital must be allocated to obtaining resources, the production efficiency of capital decreases and the capital-output ratio
goes up.

Output per capita is the single force acting here to slow the
population explosion. As output per capita increases, the desired family size declines, the birth rate goes down (Figure 5)
and population growth typically decreases. The influence of

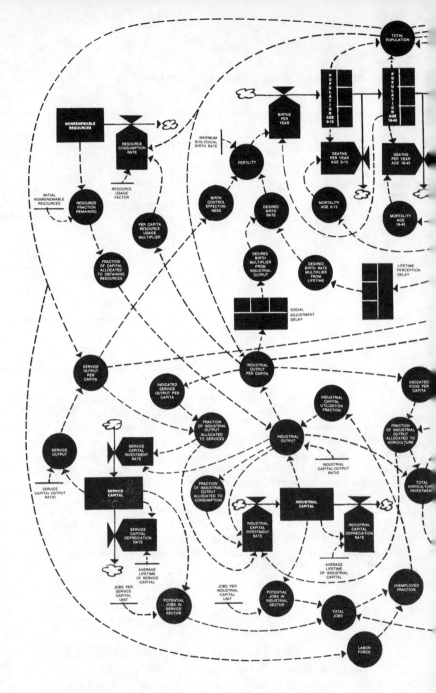

Figure 6 THE WORLD MODEL

The entire world model is represented here by a flow diagram in formal
System Dynamics notation. Levels, or physical quantities that can be measured directly, are indicated by rectangles ▬, rates that influence
those levels by valves ▷◁, and auxiliary variables that influence the

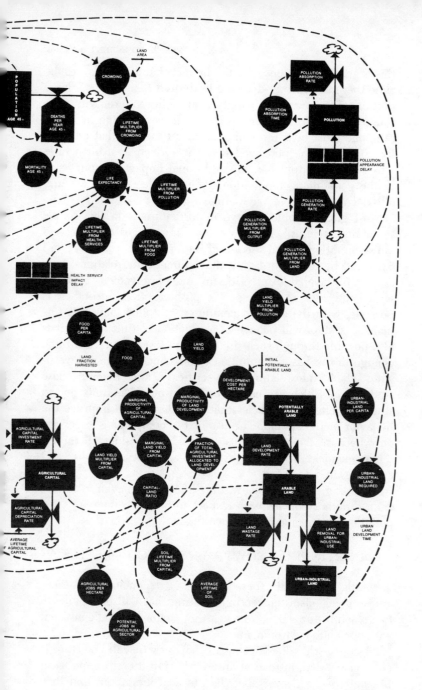

rate equations by circles ●. Time delays are indicated by sections within rectangles ▬▬▬. Real flows of people, goods, money, etc. are shown by solid arrows ──▶ and causal relationships by broken arrows ---▶. Clouds ☁ represent sources or sinks that are not important to the model behavior.

this is accelerated somewhat by the fact that as death rates decline there is a further decrease in desired family size. A large portion of the world's parents bear children primarily as a source of support in their old age. If there is a high mortality rate, one must bear three or four sons to insure that one will live. Thus, as the perceived death rate decreases, birth rates also decline. Output has one additional impact. Output leads to the generation of pollution. Pollution decreases food, and also decreases the average lifetime.

Most global problems have important roots in this simple set of interactions.[1] There are four advantages to collecting our assumptions about the world into a formal model (Figure 6). First, by explicitly listing the assumed interrelations, they are readily available for criticism and improvement by those with knowledge in each specific problem area. Second, it is possible, with the aid of a computer, to follow how this formalized system will behave as a function of time. Third, it is also possible through such simulation to test the effect of some change in the basic assumptions, and hence one may investigate which interrelations are critical (and deserve close study) and which are not. Fourth, the model permits one to study the effects of policies that he believes will improve the behavior of the system. The use of the computer is necessary only because the calculations required to consider all the interconnections between variables are very tedious and time-consuming.

Figures 7, 8 and 9 show the differing behavior resulting from different policies with respect to natural resource usage, pollution control and capital investment.

CONTINUED GROWTH LEADS TO COLLAPSE

Simulation runs like these have led us to conclude that there are no mechanisms currently operating that will bring growth to a smooth stop when we reach the maximum level consistent with our finite environment.

Of course this does not mean that growth will not stop. It only means that, instead of an orderly transition to some feasible state, we will overshoot the physical limitations and then be forced into a traumatic retrenchment to a level of popula-

Figure 7 WORLD MODEL STANDARD RUN

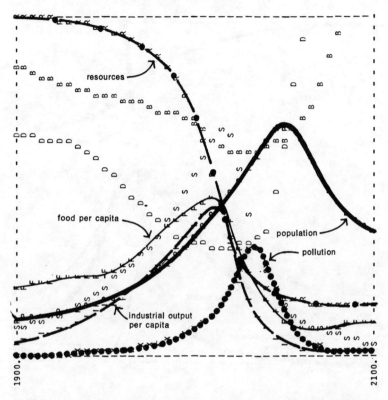

The "standard" world model run assumes no major change in the physical, economic, or social relationships that have historically governed the development of the world system. All variables plotted here follow historical values from 1900 to 1970. Food, industrial output, and population grow exponentially until the rapidly diminishing resource base forces a slowdown in industrial growth. Because of natural delays in the system, both population and pollution continue to increase for some time after the peak of industrialization. Population growth is finally halted by a rise in the death rate due to decreased food and medical services.

tion and industrialization that can be supported by our physical environment—which by then will be sorely depleted. For once we exceed a constraint, tremendous pressures will develop to halt the growth. If it so happens that we begin exceeding the absorptive capacity for pollution, the pressures

Figure 8 WORLD MODEL WITH "UNLIMITED" RESOURCES

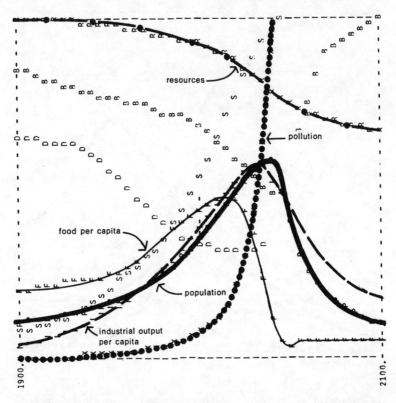

*The problem of resource depletion in the world model system is eliminated by two assumptions: first, that "unlimited" nuclear power will double the resource reserves that can be exploited and, second, that nuclear energy will make extensive programs of recycling and substitution possible. If these changes are the **only** ones introduced in the system, growth is stopped by rising pollution.*

will take the form of radical increases in death rates due to impurities in food, water and air, decreases in crops and fish catches due to similar reductions in plant and animal life, and significant reduction in the effectiveness of investment due to high costs of controlling the increased pollution in all *input*-factors. These pressures will mount until the population and industrialization finally involuntarily start to decline, and the

Figure 9 WORLD MODEL WITH "UNLIMITED" RESOURCES AND POLLUTION CONTROLS

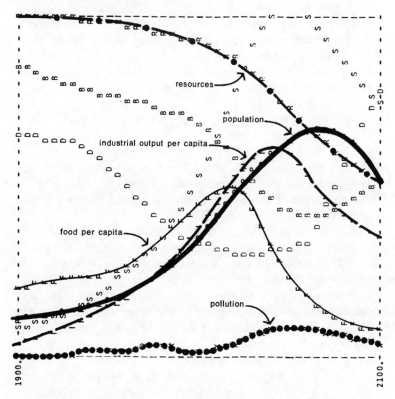

A further technological improvement is added to the world model in 1975 to avoid the resource depletion and pollution problems of previous model runs. Here we assume that pollution generation per unit of industrial and agricultural output can be reduced to one-fourth of its 1970 value. Resource policies are the same as those in figure 8. These changes allow population and industry to grow until the limit of arable land is reached. Food per capita declines, and industrial growth is also slowed as capital is diverted to food production.

pressures will only cease when levels are reached that are acceptable to the physical environment. It is like the explosion of an algae population in a nutritious medium: growth stops only when the algae are poisoned by their own wastes. And equally important: when this occurs, the population not only stops growing but enters a precipitous decline.

If we attempt to continue growth by removing one set of pressures—for instance, by increasing the food output through high-yield grains—we alleviate the situation only until we encounter the next constraint. It's like growing taller in a room with infinitely many ceilings: one does not *solve* the problem by removing the first ceiling upon contact, nor by removing the second, third and so on. Because the globe is finite, physical growth will always bring us into conflict.

THE SHORT-TERM OBJECTIVE FUNCTION

Thus we are faced with the fact that continuation of current growth practices will inevitably lead us to some sort of collapse, with a subsequent decrease in the cultural and economic options of the human race. The natural question to ask is: What shall we do?

It is important to realize that our answer to this question is completely dependent on our choice of criterion for what is "good." If we do not know what we want to obtain, if we don't know our "objective function," it is meaningless to try to decide what to do in a given situation. If our objective is to maximize the benefits for the people alive today, our course of action will be quite different from our actions if the goal is to maximize the benefits for all people who are going to live on our planet over the next 200 years.

At least in principle—and I am aware of the fact that this is far from being a realized principle—present human behavior is guided by the general idea that all people alive *today* are equally important and that the objective function is to maximize the total current benefits for all of these people. We have decided, at least in the Western democracies, that this objective is best served by letting each individual be free to pursue his own interest. It is assumed, very simply, that if every citizen and institution in our society acts to maximize his own position in the short term, the society as a whole will benefit.

This acceptance of "The Invisible Hand" has, however, introduced a strong emphasis on short-term benefits in our societies. When an action will bring both benefits and eventual costs, individuals use the concept of net present value and discount the future implications so that they can determine whether an action is profitable—and hence should be taken. The result of this procedure is that we essentially assign zero value to anything happening more than twenty years from now. In other words, actions will be taken although their cost to society twenty years hence is going to be enormous— just because the benefits are larger than the costs in the short run (e.g. over the next decade).

If we choose to adhere strictly to the objective of maximizing the short-term rewards of the present generation, there are in fact no environmental trade-offs to be made where we will have to weigh current benefits against future costs. In this case we would simply continue as before, maximizing the current benefits and neglecting any future costs that will result.

The question about use or non-use of DDT, for example, would be easily resolved. The fact that today 1.3 billion people can live in safety from malaria due to DDT would grossly outweigh the costs inflicted upon future generations through our continued use of the chemical—for instance in the form of inedible fish.

It is only this short-term objective function that can lead to the currently accepted conclusion that the value of an additional human being is infinite. The severe restrictions his existence will impose on the choices and perhaps even the lives of future generations—because of his consumption of nonrenewable natural resources and his contribution to the destruction of the life support system of the globe—is completely neglected.

Thus we see that adherence to the short-term objective function resolves very simply all trade-offs between current benefits and future cost. Of course we will be left with the ordinary trade-offs among people alive today—for instance, the choice between denying the firm upstream freedom to dump waste in the river and denying those who live downstream pure drinking water. But these short-term conflicts are not relevant to our discussion, because we *do* have mechanisms in our society to resolve conflicts between two people alive today.

We do *not* have, however, mechanisms, or even moral guidelines, for resolving conflicts between the current population and the people of the future. And our simulation model demonstrates that the present preoccupation with what seems pleasant or profitable in the short run fuels the growth that is finally going to make the world overshoot some physical constraint, forcing us—and especially our descendants—into a period of abrupt and significant changes.

THE LONG-TERM OBJECTIVE FUNCTION

It is, however, possible to change the objective function—in the same way as Christianity changed the objective of man from selfish gratification to consideration for the welfare of all people living at the same point in time.

We could change again, and for example adopt as our cardinal philosophy the rule that no man or institution in our society may take any action that decreases the economic and social options of those who will live on the planet over the next 100 years. Probably only religion has the moral force to bring such a change.

Basically we are facing only one ethical question in the impending global crisis. This is to decide on whether we want to continue to let our actions be guided by the short-term objective function, or whether we should adopt a longer-term perspective. In other words: the ethical question confronting global society today is deciding on the length of the time period used to compare costs and benefits of current actions.

It is my feeling that the moral and ethical leaders of our societies should adopt the goal of increasing the time-horizon implicit in mankind's activities—that is, introducing the longer-term objective function that maximizes the benefit for those living today, subject to the constraint that it does not decrease the economic and social options of those who will inherit this globe, our children and grandchildren.

This goal is of course not completely foreign to contemporary society. People in general feel some responsibility for the lives of their children, and the long-term objective function seems to be the value implicit in the actions of conservationists. However, ultimately it must be present in *all* of our activities—as it is said to have been in the tribal groups of Sierra Leone where nothing could be done to the jungle that would leave it unfit for the use of *all* future generations.

A LASTING SOLUTION

Assuming that we accept the long-term objective function as the guideline for our actions, what will we do about the approaching collision between our growing societies and the physical limits of the earth?

As soon as we are committed to the creation of a long-term, viable world system, our most important task becomes avoiding the trauma connected with actually exceeding any of the globe's physical limitations—food production capability, pollution absorption capacity or resource supply. This can only be done through a deliberate decision to stop physical growth. We must engineer a smooth transition to a non-growth situation—a "global equilibrium," a steady state—that is in accordance with our globe's physical limits. We must ourselves halt the growth by developing and employing legal, economic or religious pressures as substitutes for those pressures that would otherwise have been exerted by nature to halt the physical growth.

By starting now we may still be able to *choose* the set of pressures we prefer to employ in stopping population and capital growth. We cannot avoid pressures. As we continue growing, nature will supply counter forces—forces that *will* rise until growth stops. However, a deliberate choice of the least objectionable counter-forces is likely to leave intact many more of our fundamental, long-term objectives than is the blind and random action of natural forces such as starvation, social breakdown and so on.

The steady state is first of all defined by constant population and capital—i.e. by having a constant number of people and a constant amount of physical objects for all of the future. A second requirement is equally important. Since we want to create a system capable of existing for a long time, the state of equilibrium must be characterized by minimal consumption of non-renewable materials and by minimal emissions of non-degradable waste, in order to maximize the time before resources are depleted and to avoid a critical overload on the environment.

One possible way of achieving such a world equilibrium is depicted in Figure 10. Many different paths to equilibrium do

Figure 10 STABILIZED WORLD MODEL 1

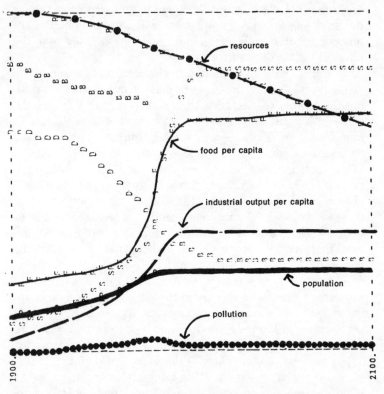

This run shows the creation of an equilibrium state sustainable far into the future. Technological policies include resource recycling, pollution control devices, increased lifetime of all forms of capital, and methods to restore eroded and infertile soil. Value changes include increased emphasis on food and services rather than on industrial production. Births are set equal to deaths and industrial capital investment equal to capital depreciation. Equilibrium value of industrial output per capita is three times the 1970 world average.

exist, however, and the choice depends on our objectives. For instance: do we want many people at a low material standard of living or few at a higher? Do we want fancy food or just the minimum daily ration of calories, protein and vitamins?

In this equilibrium mode of human civilization, science and technology will be busily developing ways of constructing products that last a long time, do not emit pollution and can be easily recycled. Competition among individual firms may very well continue, the only difference being that the total market for material goods will no longer expand. In work, emphasis will be on repair and maintenance rather than on new production.

Although equilibrium implies non-growth of all *physical* activities, this will not be the case for cultural activities. Freed from preoccupation with material goods, people may throw their energy into development of the arts and sciences, into the enjoyment of unspoiled nature and into meaningful interactions with their fellow man. The production of services may flourish.

THE DISTRIBUTION OF WEALTH AND RESPONSIBILITY

Stopping the population explosion is becoming increasingly more accepted as an important task to be accomplished as fast as possible, but what about stopping physical growth? Do I really suggest that we shall deliberately restrict our production and leave the world's poor in their miserable present situation?

This is not what is being suggested. Overall growth must finally stop, but that does not preclude redistribution of the world's existing material wealth. In practice, what this might mean is that the developed world deliberately stops its growth and possibly even lets itself "shrink" somewhat, while the developing world is allowed (or helped) to grow economically to an acceptable, but still sustainable level. Initially it will be the developed world that has to take the lead towards equilibrium —however, the developing world will have serious responsibilities in attempting to stop its rapidly growing population.

Some may think that we should stay with the goal of maximizing physical growth for quite awhile, simply because we are still so *very* far from having attained the Utopia where everything is plentiful for everyone. However, before making this choice, one should remember that a continued reliance on short-term objectives and continued growth only makes it certain that there will be no acceptable future—for *any* country.

In other words: such a Utopia does not exist, and striving towards it is futile.

Also it should be made quite clear that the type of growth we have experienced over the last century in *no* way has resulted in increased equality among the world's people. To the contrary, growth in its present form simply widens the gap between the rich and poor, as can be seen from Figure 11.

An end to overall growth, however, might very well ultimately lead to an equitable distribution of wealth throughout the world—because one would no longer be able to accept material inequalities in the present under the (false) pretense that they would be removed through future growth. This is of course not to say that the state of equilibrium will be without its problems—mainly political and ethical. Or in the words of H. E. Daly, the American economist:

> For several reasons the important issues of the stationary state will be distribution, not production. The problem of relative shares can no longer be avoided by appeals to growth. The argument that everyone should be happy as long as his absolute share of the wealth increases, regardless of his relative share, will no longer be available. The stationary state would make fewer demands on our environmental resources, but much greater demands on our moral resources.[2]

But these political problems have solutions and we may only hope that we manage to solve them. Thus it should appear that the idea of stopping overall physical growth on our planet is far from being an attempt by the rich countries to divert attention from "the" issue—namely economic development—to the protection of "their" environment. Rather, equilibrium is a necessity if mankind wants to have an equitable future on this small, fragile planet.

THE GOLDEN AGE

Only an orderly transfer into an equilibrium will save us from the tumult of an environmental crisis, and again put the human race into harmony with the world's ecosystem.

Equilibrium could permit the development of an unprece-

Figure 11 ECONOMIC GROWTH RATES

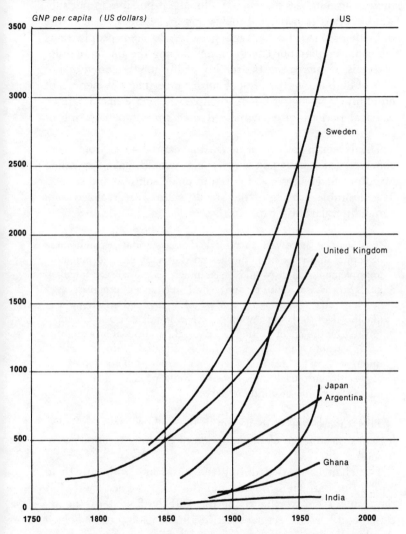

The economic growth of individual nations indicates that differences in exponential growth rates are widening the economic gap between rich and poor countries.

SOURCE: Simon Kuznets, *Economic Growth of Nations* (Cambridge, Mass.: Harvard University Press, 1971).

dented golden age for humanity. Freedom from ever-increasing numbers of people will make it possible to put substantial effort into the self-realization and development of the individual. Instead of struggling merely to keep people alive, we could employ our energy in developing the human culture —that is, in increasing the quality of life for the individual to a level high above the present subsistence. The few periods of equilibrium in the past—for example, the 300 years of Japan's classical period—often witnessed such profound flowering of the arts.

The freedom from ever-increasing capital—i.e., from more concrete, cars, dams and skyscrapers—would make it possible even for our great-grandchildren to enjoy solitude and silence. The desirable aspects of the steady state were realized long ago. John Stuart Mill wrote in 1857:

> It is scarcely necessary to remark that a stationary condition of capital and population implies no stationary state of human improvement. There would be as much scope as ever for all kinds of mental culture, and moral and social progress; as much room for improving the art of living and much more likelihood of its being improved, when minds cease to be engrossed by the art of getting on. Even the industrial arts might be as earnestly and as successfully cultivated, with this sole difference, that instead of serving no purpose but the increase of wealth, industrial improvements would produce their legitimate effect, that of abridging labor.[3]

This, then, is the state of equilibrium, which seems to be the logical consequence of the adoption of the long-term objective function.

The changes needed during the transition from growth to equilibrium are tremendous, and the time is very short. But the results seem worth striving for, and the first step—the acceptance of a long-term objective function—is one in which the churches have always been a leader.

Footnotes

1. For further information, see Donella H. Meadows, Dennis L. Meadows, Jørgen Randers, William W. Behrens, *The Limits to*

Growth, Universe Books, New York, 1972; and Jay W. Forrester, *World Dynamics,* Wright-Allen Press, Cambridge, Mass., 1971.

2. Herman E. Daly in *The Patient Earth,* John Harte and Robert Socolow, eds. (New York: Holt, Rinehart and Winston), 1971.

3. John Stuart Mill, *Principles of Political Economy,* Vol. II (London: John W. Parker and Son), 1857.

TECHNOLOGY AND CONVIVIALITY

ivan illich

──────── IVAN ILLICH ────────

There is a deep desire in our culture to move toward a future that is simple and uncomplicated, where men can relate more openly and creatively to their work, their communities, their environment. The technological culture we have fashioned has given great freedoms, possibilities and luxuries, but it has not released the spirit and friendship of man; rather it has suppressed his more human capacities. The institutions and professions in our culture have often conspired to convince man that he cannot do for himself what he is perfectly capable of doing. Often society has kept from men the tools for personal and community creativity. In this essay Ivan Illich pours content and example into the more sensibly frugal life style that Randers calls for. Illich is director of the Center for Intercultural Documentation in Cuernavaca, Mexico. This lecture, submitted for discussion by the symposium, was most provocative.

TECHNOLOGY AND CONVIVIALITY

Individuals need tools to move and to dwell. They need remedies for their diseases and resources to communicate with one another. Some of these things people cannot make for themselves. They depend upon being supplied with objects and services which vary from culture to culture. Some people depend upon the supply of shoes and others upon the supply of ovens. Some need to get aspirin and others printing presses.

People do not only need to obtain things; above all they need the freedom to make the things among which they live, to give shape to them according to their own taste and to put them to use in caring for and about others. Prisoners often have access to more things and services than other members of their families, but they have no say in how things are to be made and cannot decide what to do with them. Their punishment consists in being deprived of what I shall call conviviality.

I choose the term conviviality to designate the contrary of productivity. I want it to mean autonomous and creative intercourse among persons, and intercourse of persons with their environment, and this in contrast with the conditioned and efficient response of persons to the demands made upon them by others or by their milieu. I consider conviviality individual freedom realized in mutual personal interdependence and, as such, an intrinsic ethical value. I believe that without conviviality life becomes meaningless and persons wither.

Politics is the formal structure by which a given society expresses and enforces the values it happens to accept. All present political structures, be they labelled liberal, Marxist or conservative, express and enforce productivity at the expense of conviviality. They provide goods with clients rather than people with goods. Individuals are forced to pay for and use things they do not need; they are allowed no effective part in the process of choosing, let alone producing them. Products multiply for the sake of proliferation, which keeps the process of production expanding.

A schoolroom, a hospital, an urban intersection in Czechoslovakia can hardly be distinguished from one in the United States or Turkey or Argentina. Tie-ups on the access roads to a capital do not depend on the number of cars per one hundred inhabitants; they are as bad in Rio as they are on Long Island. One shudders to think that the central lane now reserved for party bureaucrats (and emergency vehicles) in Moscow will disappear under the onslaught of products from the new Fiat factory in the Urals. And the more people in any society think that one must have a car, the less prone they are to take hitchhikers in their empty seats. Conviviality declines with rising productivity.

All politicians promise to increase the output of doctors. People come to believe that you *must* have a doctor when you have a seizure on the street. The doctor thinks he *must* have a car to get to his client or a paraprofessional to send with the ambulance. As dependence on the doctor grows, people first become frightened of the man who lies on the sidewalk with convulsions, then they become impotent in assisting him, and finally they unlearn to care. "Let George do it" comes to mean that there ought to be some specialized institution that can deal with this "case."

Since the mid-sixties everyone has begun to be conscious of the way in which proliferation of goods is spoiling the physical environment. Rising productivity in the supply of manufactured goods has irreversible results in depletion and pollution, because the world is a limited system and cannot support an unlimited physical sub-system. But the inevitable accumulation of durable junk in a constantly obsolescent society is so obvious that I do not want to labor the point now.

What I do want to call attention to is a parallel process in the service sector: the fact that rising productivity and supply of services results in the irrecuperable loss of conviviality. It deprives persons of their own potency, of their freedom, and society of the memory that these could once have been treasured.

NEW POLITICS

What I want to propose is a radically new politics, a politics that will enforce the individual's right to use only what he needs, to play an increasing part as an individual in its production and to an environment so simple and transparent that all men will have access to all the things that are useful to care for themselves and for others most of the time. Such politics would have as their major goal an inversion of present institutional purposes.

The basic malfunction of our present institutions is not due to bad management, nor to official dishonesty, nor to a technological lag. It is due to a basic reversal of the relative functions of productivity and conviviality. The more efficient the manager and the more fastidious the bureaucrat and the greater the power of the tool over which they have dominion, the more certain can the client be that he gets what is on the label. But he can also be sure that the institution will deny him all rights to do it for himself. Frozen foods from all countries in all seasons guarantee that fresh food from the neighborhood will become a luxury even in season.

The reversal of institutional purposes is equally typical for societies where the consumer is told that he is king as it is for societies where the producer is told that he is in the saddle. An increasing expectancy level for commodities of predictable quality decreases my dependence on another man's kindness, which might surprise and strengthen me.

The relative preponderance of productive over convivial purpose in institutions is also used as a measurement of the level of development a society has achieved. Societies in which the majority of the people depend on the personal whim, kindness or skill of another for most of their goods and services are called "underdeveloped," while those in which living has been transformed into a process of ordering from an all-encompassing store-catalogue are called "advanced." Every aspect of these advanced societies (be they capitalist, Marxist or whatever) has become part of a larval system for escalating production and the consumption that is necessary to justify and pay for it.

For this reason, criticism of bad management, official dishonesty and technological lag simply distract public attention from the issue. Equally distracting is the suggestion that productivity pursued under the tutelage of a planning board that protects the interests of a majority would lead to less frustrating results than productivity sky-rocketing under the pressure of dissatisfied consumers. Attempts to improve the quality of products or the equity of their distribution will only increase pollution, impotency and overdetermination and rob the rich and the poor of conviviality, which is still their primary treasure.

Because I define politics as I do, I take it seriously. I believe that soon, as a result of the recognition of frustrations, the time will be ripe for a political restructuring of the relationship between production and consumption, and certainly for the reverse of what Marx foresaw and hoped for in 1843, "a society full of useful things and useless people." I look forward to a society, and so to a political structure, that will enable creative persons to meet their needs as producers and as users.

I believe that we are now near the point at which the frustration created by several of these institutions will become unbearable. This happens as the attempts to improve either the quality of the product or the equity with which they serve their clients proves futile. At this point the political atmosphere will be ripe to redefine the purpose that institutions should serve in a technological age. Present institutions provide clients with predetermined goods. Desirable institutions ought to enable creative people to meet their own needs. Present institutions have made commodities out of health, education, housing, transportation and welfare. We need arrangements that permit modern man to engage in the activities of healing and health maintenance, learning and teaching, moving and dwelling. I propose to set a legal limit to the tooling of society in such a way that the toolkit necessary to conviviality will be accessible for the autonomous use of a maximum number of people. In other words, we make conviviality the criterion for the level of productivity of society's tooling.

BACKGROUND OF THE PROBLEM

The progress of science is frequently blamed for this functional shift of institutions from frameworks for action to factories of goods, a shift that in several European languages is reflected in a simultaneous linguistic shift from verb to substantive for the designation of their purpose. No doubt it is true that scientific discoveries are now used to render supply-funnels for more copious commodities that crowd tool shops for independent enterprise off the scene. But all this is not the fault of scientific input in itself. Rather it is the result of the intent with which science is applied. Science could be equally well used to increase the toolkit available to every man, allowing individuals and transient gatherings of associates to

constantly recreate their environment with undreamt-of freedom and formerly unthinkable self-expression. In 1945 30
percent of all houses in Massachusetts were owner-built, at
least to some extent; today the figure is down to 10 percent.
Certainly new materials and handy tools could have made
possible an increase rather than a decline in housing as an activity expressed by those who want to live there. The number
of medicines and knowledge about their usefulness and their
side-effects has grown immensely in the last two generations.
Yet during the same time information about them has become
increasingly restricted; the Merck Manual (of drugs) is now
off the market, and increasingly medicines are considered
mysterious and dangerous unless prescribed by a doctor, who
often does his prescribing over the phone. Books have become
cheaper to produce than they ever were before. Yet the number of books purchased yearly by a high school graduate in
the United States has fallen constantly over the last two decades and is now lower than in any comparably developed
country. One would think that this would lead to the use of
other educational devices outside of "programs" offered in
school or over television. Instead the populace is so thor-
oughly trained to desire only what is packaged and channeled
through a delivery hook-up, that most of what all citizens
know is acquired in audiences numbered by the millions when
a television station finds it profitable to program it.

If science were used to increase the power of individuals to
create their own milieu and to care for each other, this would
give the leverage through which institutional purposes could
be inverted. It would make it possible to substitute the question: "What tools do people need and what do they have to
know if they want to heal or care for those in the process of
being healed?" for the current concern with the delivery of
anonymous health services. But such an inversion of institutional purpose cannot be the result of market pressure, nor can
the managers of our industries, who are used to wielding the
power by which commodities are provided to people, be expected to turn into switchboard managers of a market. The
decision to limit the use of technology to increase productivity
for the benefit of industry, and increase the use of technology
in a way that actually competes with and contradicts the

ideals of an industrial society, is the most important challenge for radical politics and legislation during the seventies. The translation of this social imperative into political terms can be clearly projected.

THE POLITICAL CHALLENGE

It has become almost senseless to contrast the political left with the right. You cannot tell a liberal from a conservative unless he wears a button. The economists of socialist and capitalist countries say the same things with different rhetoric. The public budget of rich and poor countries mainly shows quantitative differences. New politics has come to mean new ways of getting more of the same.

Present political platforms appeal to their following by proposing a set of goods and services the economy will provide if and when the party gets into power. Each party presents a different profile of minimum quanta, which it promises to provide for everybody. Each party tailors its profile of promised minima to the probable consensus of a particular group of voters. By doing so, politics becomes a process by which the voters agree on what is insufficient, leave undetermined what amount of consumption of public resources will be considered as good enough, do not impose any limits on what ought to be excessive—as long as its use by a person can somehow be justified as being for the common good.

The alternative to such a political platform would be one that offers a profile of upper limits on the resources that any individual may use either in his own or in the public interest: something that seems to be a logical antecedent to the promise of a guaranteed minimum quantum for everybody. Such alternate politics would generate a consensus on what a society considers enough for one person, and good enough for everybody over a long period of time. Present politics seeks agreement on what ought to be considered insufficient and refuses to define what ought to be good enough. Desirable politics ought to seek an agreement about the profile of commodities that a majority considers more than good enough.

The American and Soviet histories are parallel in this regard. In February of 1931 the United States depression hit bottom; Trotsky and Bucharing had been defeated and Stalin launched the Soviet Union on the road of ruthless industrialization. He gave as the reason why: "We are 50 or 100 years behind the advanced countries. We must make good the lag in 10 years."

Stalin translated "the control over the means of production" to mean the increase of productivity by new means used for the control of the producer. Since then, a socialist policy is one that serves the productivity of a socialist country.

Stalin's interpretation of this fundamental Marxist goal has since then served as a form of blackmail against socialists and the left. This can be seen clearly in relation to formerly colonial countries, to which Lenin assigned a "revolutionary" role. Stalin's principle permits the interpretation of whatever increases the amount of schooling, the road system and the productivity of extraction and manufacture as revolutionary. To be on the left has come to mean either to champion the nation that lags in production or to help the minority that lags in consumption to catch up.

The rebirth of a meaningful left, both national and international, depends on the ability to learn to distinguish between control of the means and mode of production in the service of people and control of people for the purpose of raising output, followed by worry about fair distribution.

The crisis of the left has reinforced the crisis of socialism. It cannot be overcome unless we gain insight into the fatal correlation between rising productivity and the modernization of the class structure, of exploitation and of poverty. Only if we learn to distinguish control of the means of production from control of people for the purpose of increasing productivity, only then can we find the common element for an international left. The enormous potential of production that science, quite recently, has made possible, renders social control of the distribution of work and benefits illusory unless the control also extends to "what" is produced and "if" it is needed. Such a social inversion of goals, if it is successfully expressed in a political formulation of maxima rather than minima, will demand a comparable inversion of the major institutions of society: education, health-care, transportation, housing and so on.

Political power is now used to increase the production of

commodities. In an alternate concept of politics, the power arising from consensus would be used overwhelmingly to set the limits within which modern tools may enable the individual of a political community to satisfy his needs.

I hope to deal with a variety of reasons that make it difficult to make self-limitation within boundaries the condition for the establishment of a political community, especially if these boundaries are of more than a territorial nature. Our political imagination is mesmerized by alternatives for the *production* of more things for more people and thus paralyzed when we try to focus on a possible inversion of political goals. New and radical politics means moving the need for upper limits into the center-stage of our public discourse. Nothing less will lead to the transformation of our institutions from producers of commodities to frameworks for individual action, from elements of a well-ordered system to guardians of increased freedom of action.

THE TASK OF INSTITUTIONAL INVERSION: THE SCHOOLS

There are strategic reasons for choosing "de-schooling" as the first step in a more general program of institutional inversion. Most people have school behind them. The world's majority know that they have been irremediably excluded from satisfactory schooling. Others who did go through a "good" school know that they have been hurt in the process. And finally most who were benefitted in some way by school know that they did not learn in school what helped them to do their jobs. Whatever school contributed to their success was probably not the subject matter they were taught. Agreement on the need to disestablish schools can be reached.

In previous articles written for the *New York Review of Books*, I have shown that education based on *output* of a school system is bound to fail. Inevitably the economic costs of such education grow faster than the gross national product that they are supposed to boost. This is true for all countries, rich and poor, during the sixties. Inevitably more people are degraded as dropouts or are stamped below par than are given the certificate that imputes to them superior productivity and claims to privilege. Quantifiable education produced by schools serves as a rationale to correlate productivity and income on a worldwide basis. It is also inevitable that a society that defines education as a commodity discourages acquiring learning from participation in everyday life, and creates a rationale for an environment in which fewer people have access to the facts and tools that shape their lives. This is so because information becomes shrouded in a secrecy that dissolves only for those who pass through an appropriate graded ritual of initiation. Tools are made scarce and reserved to the few to whom information is reserved—supposedly for the purpose of making their products plentiful. In summary, I have shown that schools, by creating a hierarchy of knowledge-capitalists, whether the particular society considers itself socialist or not, alienate men from other men by reducing interaction in the relationships between professionals and their clients, and also alienate man from his environment by making the consumer into a marginal participant in the processes by which his needs are satisfied.

I also hope I have shown that the translation of education into the process of accumulating certified shares of the knowledge stock serves to ration access to the scarce upper levels of a consumer society and to justify a technocratic organization that each year produces more expensive and more scarce goods, that in turn are primarily reserved for the knowledge capitalists who hold a high rank in the technocracy.

I have argued that the present crisis in education will only be accentuated by a further increase in the output of schools. The crisis in education can be solved only through an inversion of the institutional structure of agencies that now serve it. It can be overcome only if the present schools, with or without walls, that prepare or authorize programs for students, are replaced by new institutions that are more like libraries and matching services that empower the learner to find access to the tools and encounters that he needs to learn to fit his own choices.

Schools enable a teacher to establish classes of subjects and to impute the need for them to classes of people called pupils. The inverse of schools would be opportunity webs that permit individuals to state their present interest and seek to match it.

THE HEALTH SERVICES MONOLITH

It is relatively easier for an adult to imagine a world without schools than it is for him to forswear the need of a hospital, but to do the first might lead to the second. It is evident that the structural inversion of our major institutions will either happen for several of them more or less at the same time or it will not happen at all. It cannot happen as long as people have not become aware of the illusion that modern economics fosters. Once the veil of illusion has been penetrated all major institutions as presently constituted become vulnerable. As the school undergoes inversion, possibly the health services monolith is the next most accessible target, with transportation and housing becoming open to attack at the same time.

The application of such inversion of social goals through the politics of maximum rather than minimum limits would, as I shall develop further, find its expression through the inversion of the structure of the institutions that now deliver education, health welfare or other goods. The fundamental economic problem must be uncovered first.

Taboos established by economic orthodoxy paralyze our imagination when we are asked to imagine a world turned topsy turvy. A vulgar edition of post-Keynesian economic growth-mythology makes it impossible to gain people's attention when one proposes an inversion of institutional goals. Political economists now play the role formerly reserved to theologians. Their meta-mythological doctrines provide the concepts out of which the pattern of other more specialized myths are woven. Their litany is all-purpose problem solving through maximum growth.

Economists provide us with an axiom on which all their reasoning is based. This axiom states that frustration is the inevitable outcome of satisfaction and that there cannot be enough of a good thing but only more. The Council of Economic Advisors in this year's report to the President of the United States sum up: "If it is agreed that economic output is a good thing, it follows by definition that there is not enough of it." In this view man is a bottomless trash can, an incurable consumer and a compulsive producer. Productive institutions have the sole purpose of providing him with operant conditioning for the escalating exploitation that guarantees their further growth.

Not only do schools, hospitals and armies look alike everywhere in the world; the economic reasoning underlying their planning as well comes only in different shades of the same color. Nixon's advisors differ from those appointed by Brezhnev, Franco and unfortunately also Castro basically in that they are less candid in the statement of their metaphysics.

The Council of Economic Advisors (CEA) acknowledges that there might be a limit to the ills growth could cure: "The growth of GNP has its costs and beyond some point these are not worth paying." But the CEA does not waste any effort toward determining this point. In fact growth-economics provides no method of pinpointing the level at which planned costs outgrow planned benefits, since both are subsumed under the same category of "institutional outputs." Therefore all the Council does is to state that further growth cannot be stopped: "The existing propensities of the population and the policies of the government constitute claims upon GNP itself that can only be met by rapid economic growth." The CEA declares itself incompetent either to challenge the de facto dictatorship of the consumer or change the policies enacted by those industrial managers whom the consumer has elected to exercise his dictatorship.

Western economists explain the need for open-ended growth as the consequence of the unlimited wants of consumers, which the party wanting to stay in power has to meet. Socialist economists explain the same need for unlimited growth as the manifestation of historical progress. In fact the advancement of a society to higher forms of production justifies the dictatorship of a victorious proletariat which the party officials represent. They presume to dictate higher production for its own sake, rather than for the presumed satisfaction of their constituency. The Western economist speaks in the name of Ford and Ford's captive consumer-mass. The growth maniac socialist speaks in the name of a producer-class and advocates that this class aspire to become, as soon as possible, its most exploited client.

The health arena provides an example of concern where the self limitation of technology becomes a basic condition for reinstitution of the basic value of health care. New and radical politics are needed, and they must call for upper limits of per capita consumption as the center of our worldwide aspirations. A human technology must be the goal replacing the present technology that subordinates human needs to ever-increasing productivity.

INSURANCE: THE MARKET AS A GAMBLE

Modern nations tend to look alike in at least three ways: they use identical tools, they use the same toolkit and they use the same methods to distribute their output. Schools are tools to produce education; hospitals are tools to produce health services; and mass-circulation papers or programs are tools to provide daily information. These tools depend on each other. The growth of the medical profession depends on the output level of medical schools, just as the number of medical schools depends on the availability of teaching hospitals. Finally, access to the more costly services of both hospitals and schools depends on some form of legalized gambling. The medical profession, its place among other professions, and the lottery that gives access to its services differ from country to country only in name and in niceties, as flags differ from each other.

Under President Johnson, a religious war about the name of the medical gamble came to an end in the United States. Americans agreed to call their distribution system an "insurance plan." Since then different model-plans have been designed and are now proposed to the public so that it may choose one of them as a monopoly. Whichever model wins, the benefit accrues to the medical profession. Politics thus becomes the arena to play the tune, on the same set of instruments, that each party hopes will bewitch the majority. The 1972 elections might become the first in history staked on a popularity contest between two publicity campaigns, both organized to provide a monopoly for the same industrial complex called "health."

It is the nature of national health insurance to channel tax resources for spending to the control of doctors. It is equally in its nature to reinforce the idea that the doctor's services are priceless, and that he alone ought to decide how much service is desirable for each patient. Compulsory health insurance is a first step toward compulsory health treatment. Until now the citizen was just considered immoral if he did not play at a lottery with an open drawing date called health insurance. In the new game, he *must* play—and the doctor's house *must* win.

When medical insurance becomes obligatory and provides access to potentially unlimited treatment—should professional reasons make it desirable—it becomes a regressive tax. Those who die quickest get least service, and those who die slowly get the most questionable service. Medical costs per capita rise steeply as death approaches. Doctors and their institutions are encouraged to concentrate their services on the clinical consolation of the dying. Insurance provides the medical profession with more resources for life-prolongation, drawn from a society that becomes less healthy in the process of producing them. Compulsory health insurance then opens the door for unending extortion by the medical profession.

All this, of course, is true only as long as no upper limit is set on the per capita outlay of public expenditure. Public control of the medical complex stands and falls with the honesty with which the need for such a limit is faced. Lay boards with the power to hire or fire doctors and set their maximum fees do control individual dishonesty; they cannot curb the hubris of a doctor who considers the death of a patient after a serious cancer operation a defeat of his profession. If doctors were trained with public resources, and treatments provided from tax-funds were restricted to a limited set of treatments, the public could control the medical industry. Without facing this decision, the discussion of alternate insurance plans that guarantee everybody a minimum and—if the doctor wants it—the infinite, is meaningless.

The physician knows that educated preventative care and self-health maintenance will add more years to the life of each of his patients than all the services he can provide. But personal modesty and common sense cannot free the doctor from the dynamics of an institutional complex that shapes his environment and that of his client. The monopoly of hospitals over the care of people who have to stay in bed is reflected in the architecture of modern homes. It has become unfeasible to

be sick at home, and embarrassing to stay there awaiting
death.

The fact is that under the pressure of the health professions
the maintenance of health, assistance in the restoration of
health after an accident or during a crisis, and finally terminal
life-prolongation have been monopolized by one industry—
somewhat in the manner in which age-specific custodial care,
certification, social initiation and instruction were packaged
together by schools. In this process the length of time during
which a person remains a patient or actual client of the doctor
by staying alive has become the most significant measurable
dimension of health. Life expectancy has become the most
cherished proof of the increase of health in a population, even
though its increase has little or nothing to do with the intake
of medical services, except among the dying.

As a result of all this, an aging population has come to
translate "health" into a life-prolonging commodity. A population thus fed on statistics has transformed aging into the consumption of lengthening life-expectancy that can be achieved
by drinking of the medical fountain of geriatrics. Even the
best of doctors will find it difficult to avoid his patient's lump-
ing together under the designation "medical care" the declin-
ing relief he can offer and the growing pain and frustration
that he can provide.

Most of the cost of medical research and services rendered
in United States hospitals goes for what can be done or is
done to patients during the last two years of their lives. Although in recent years there has been a dramatic increase in
medical costs in the United States for men over 45, their life
expectancy has increased insignificantly during the same
period. The probability that they will spend a period of time
in hospitals, asylums or homes for the aged has increased
threefold.

A society that defines medicine as the art of life-extension
deserves to be governed by economists who define themselves
as the architects of sustained and unlimited growth. Both the
medical and the economic enterprise thus conceived are the
outgrowth of an illusion suffered by people who deny the
human need for upper limits because they are compelled to
evade the necessity of facing death. A swelling GNP is the

proper idol for people who demand from their doctors not that they help them to heal them but just that they keep them alive. It is the ultimate symbol of value in a society that defines its growing anxiety in terms of its burgeoning wealth. Belief in the value of the GNP provides the final solution to the troublesome challenge—the need to measure benefits in a culture in which all that is desirable can somehow be reduced to wealth.

Psychologically, growth economics cannot be separated from a medicine that finds its principle achievements in the avoidance of death. GNP is a concept homologous with life expectancy. It represents that grand total of the market value of all benefits plus the expenditures incurred to protect society from the unwanted side-effects that result from the production of these benefits. A rising GNP gauges the state of a nation as medical bills do the health of a man.

The doctor is trained to provide increasing pains at an increasing cost, just as the economist stimulates increasing demand to produce increasing sales. Dr. Mendelsohn estimates that 90 percent of Chicago's outlay for public medicine and for treatment of clients actually increases suffering rather than healing or soothing it.

In a more rhetorical sense, the economist does provide for our society the abstract definition of its original sin, just as metaphysicians or theologians provided it for other times. The economist formulates the anthropology that fits our society in the most abstract terms, and defines man as a being who finds happiness in paying the highest possible price for his own operant conditioning to escalating frustration. Institutional output thus becomes the "good" because in Walden III, by definition, consumers *want* to increase the frustration they can obtain from it.

In many areas of everyday life, frustration grows faster than habituation to it. In some cases frustration has already reached a critical point. A wave of dissatisfaction with schools swept over some countries in the late sixties. This led the United States to the establishment of some ten thousand alternative educational centers. (In Peru the first legal attempt to disestablish schools will only free the present public disenchantment with industrial complexes less sacred than school.) In the meanwhile, before frustration reaches this critical level in regard to health, transportation, food-processing or housing, improvement of the institutions set up to provide for man will still be sought with two forms of "modernization."

THE "CONSUMERIST" AND "TECHNOSOPHIST" PROPOSALS

The advocates of modernization as the remedy for our institutions' crisis take two distinct reactionary roads. Each claims to lead through a revolution, and each in fact supports the *status quo*. Each of these so-called revolutions shifts the blame for the dysfunction of our institutions onto a different scapegoat and neither indicts the institutional purpose itself. The first so-called revolution speaks for the consumer, and blames the price and the quality of commodities on the manufacturer. Its proponents would like to take over Ford's departments of design and of pricing. The promoters of the second, the scientific or technological revolution, go a step further, to a point of myth-making that justifies calling their proposals "technosophic." They want, for instance, to achieve a breakthrough in the entire transportation industry that would provide them with more speed, and they do not care if they get it with or without cars. In more general terms, they propose to make our institutions serve their present ultimate purposes by providing them with more powerful tools.

I will show that each of these two revolutions advocates a more thorough espousal of our present world view, in which needs can be satisfied only by tangible or intangible commodities that we consume. Each of the two movements provides new legitimacy for the present mode of production that I have already described as operational reinforcement of the consumer's willingness to accept hardship to get diminishing, though more ardently pursued, satisfaction.

First, "Naderism" or the counter-revolution of the consumer. Cars are costly. They are unsafe. They do pollute. It is easy to blame the car manufacturer for the high price, the unreliable performance and the unchecked side-effects. It is expedient to organize frustrated consumers, even though at first this is dangerous, as Nader had to learn, and ultimately futile.

Disciplined addicts can force the underworld to peddle pure drugs. They cannot blame the junkie for selling a narcotic. The leader of the consumer revolt of the future might ride to the presidency on the prototype of a durable, non-polluting family plane. I imagine that he will smoke no more than ten filter cigarettes and advocate a "pure drug law" applicable to all commodities. He will campaign on the platform that the way to have your cake and eat it too is to make it grow not only bigger but sweeter. If the manufacturers of cars, of medical services or of professional teaching were enlightened in their own self-interest, they would support a crusade that does their consumer research for them. Ownership of a car does guarantee the right to move. If the roads are good, it guarantees the right to move fast. But this is no more guarantee for good locomotion than access to a hospital is a guarantee for medical care. Just as in the case of health, more goods can mean less benefits. The higher the speed at which a man habitually moves, the greater the amount of time he uses to get from one place to another today. In 1948 the Interstate Highway system opened for traffic. Since then the percentage of vehicles travelling faster than 60 miles per hour on all main rural roads in the United States has tripled from 16 to 45 percent. The time spent by each American in a car has grown by 50 percent and the time he has spent on the go by other means has increased even more. The maximum speed occasionally available to the member of a society is an indicator of the amount of time spent travelling. Americans spend more time travelling than Poles, and Poles spend more time travelling than Brazilians, just as the member of the jet set spends more time away from home than an ordinary citizen. Cheaper, safer and non-polluting cars travelling on wider and straighter roads at higher speeds would enable their owners to spend more time safely packaged on the go. If Ford is blamed for undesirable cars, it will produce desirable cars. But Ford cannot be blamed for the fact that the increased output of cars increases the distresses of transportation.

The technosophic counterrevolution can be called the Buckminster Fuller syndrome, whose exponents blame the distressing nature of transportation on a conspiracy between Mr. Ford and his clients. They rightly claim that this unholy alliance for mutual exploitation keeps cars on the road and builds more roads with the taxpayers' money. These technosophs would like to do away with cars in order to improve transportation. For instance, they would like to see "future gravitrains, falling of their own weight along underground channels and then swooping up again on a combination of their own momentum and pneumatic air . . . all of which would be practical with the development of cheap laser tunnelling." This idea comes from the Secretary of Transportation of the United States, John Volpe. Proposals for public transportation, while discrediting the car, support the commitments of the society to provide more speed at all cost.

Some technosophs are simple technocrats; they are all the men on duty in Washington and Moscow. They provide their employers with more power or profits and maintain their legitimacy by claiming that this power is used to serve the majority.

Others describe themselves as the prophets of a man-made paradise; these call themselves techno-anarchists. They have fallen victim to the illusion that it is possible to socialize the technocratic imperative. They would make their followers believe that the maximum technically possible is not simply the maximum desirable for a few, but that it can also provide everybody with maximum benefits at minimum cost. Of course this is true, but only if the client wants the specific thing the technosoph tells him he wants.

The spokesmen for the consumer and the technosoph are both reactionary, but the latter more profoundly so. A consumer revolution succeeds if the consumer gets what he needs from the shelf of a supermarket, from the docket of a court or from the catalogue of a university. Its success is the result of a conspiracy between salesmen and customer to provide good air-conditioners, useful degrees and properly labelled drugs and to control the shareholder. As durable junk accumulates in and out of use, the consumer still maintains real options. People may prefer clean air while bicycling to work and avoid highways where survival depends on air conditioning. Employers may accept competence acquired in apprenticeship in lieu of certificates proving attendance at classes. Organized consumers, students or welfare recipients provide a messy, though effective, support for a chaotic, but powerful production system. The legal recognition of their sundry demands reinforces the legal protection of the producers. The consumer can have a kind of victory, although only a temporary one.

Any political success of technosophic establishment, however, represents a step forward into a world where basic choices are fewer. Such a success is always the result of collusion between government and an industrial complex; a conspiracy between a particular group of consumers and a particular industry is not sufficient to support its cost. Whenever a technosophic "solution" is adopted, this means that the party in power has made commitments for the nation far beyond its mandate to govern. It has also decided what shall be made feasible on the advice of some scientific group holding secret knowledge of what is possible at an escalating cost. The adoption of a "technological" solution means a political commitment without recourse to a vote.

Once minimum speed is guaranteed to commuters, each person could be forced to use it, whether he likes it or not, as witness the minimum allowable speed now on many highways. The pattern that urbanization takes would impose the demand, without the need for a new breed of officers pressing truant commuters into a train. From now on, each victory for a new "system" will be equivalent to a move towards a society in which each man is encapsulated in multiple compulsory insurance of his consumption. The government would make sure that he gets the speed, housing, medical care or constant reschooling needed to progress. Each of these steps would require another enormous investment borrowed from the future and would amount to a new reinforcement of our present mode of production. This, of course, goes far beyond simple consumer protection; it means mandatory consumption and addiction to the straight stuff, with freedom left only to take more, not less.

To go from the present transportation-maze to gravi-trains, or from our school system to lifelong reeducation, or from the clinical labs to the diagnostic satellite, follows the same logic as progress from bombers to MIRV. To start developing the prototype is a political decision, costly, monopolistic and irreversible.

It is also an overkill of problems now created by our institutions. Just as the use of MIRV guarantees equally effective extinction (not safety) for everybody, so would lifelong re-education provide everybody with constant reassignment to his place in a meritocracy, and speedier transportation would compel everybody to longer trips, shorter stays and no way to get somewhere with their feet.

The technosoph promises to increase the output of our institutions by eliminating their current product; he provides transportation at a higher speed for everybody. But this "better" transportation means being on the move as much as possible at the highest feasible speed, rather than being at rest somewhere.

What the guarantee of minima means can best be illustrated by looking at the first profession to be entrusted with offering a minimum. Once the graduates of teachers' colleges were given a public monopoly to decide what constitutes good education, they had to use it to disqualify learning that happened outside their control. Schools became the only legitimate recipients for public funds destined for education. Inevitably learning was translated into "education," and this in turn became a commodity that could be obtained only from accredited schools. The guarantee of a minimum education was translated into the obligation to attend a minimum number of years. Soon dropouts would be denied jobs. But the guarantee does not work only against one who does not use it. The monopoly of schools over education made education into an intangible commodity. It turned the result of learning into an invisible software that is guaranteed by the code number given on the certificate. Those pupils who obtain only the legal minimum find out that they wasted their time in school; what they acquired is devalued on the market because others have more or a newer program.

Schools were not originally created with the intent of creating an industrial complex for the production of knowledge; they were meant to give everybody a chance to learn. But they became a form of compulsory insurance of every child's future productivity. The governments of the world all established the monopoly of a profession, giving them the right to decide how much of their expert treatment each citizen should get. Soon the profession could also decide how much of its treatment a concrete individual needed, and finally it could use its power to give it to him or to her. "Insurance" of minimum quanta of any service is always a form of social control that permits the manager to manipulate economic flow by determining the level of that minimum. Universal insurance thus is a way of using the gambling instinct of a population to make compulsory consumption attractive.

Nader and Fuller only reinforce what we now have. They do so on three matching levels. Their converging demands reinforce the purpose of politics, strengthen the legitimacy of further professional specialization and by this double support cement the industrial shape of all our institutions. They heighten the demand for insurance for all, for more specialized doctors or school teachers and unlimited delivery of health care services or educational software.

First, both of them support the appeal the politician now uses: the promise of a classless society made up of a luxury class with cake for all, and the moon, too, for those who reach for it. Second, both Nader and Fuller play into the hand of the professions who alone know the secret formula necessary to accomplish this magic; the formula needed for the miraculous multiplication of cakes and the formula needed to satisfy everyone with cake and a vicarious moonwalk in exchange for his freedom to do what he wants. And finally, the consumer-defender and the spokesman of unlimited production both build an airtight shell for our present world view which states that the mere fact of scientific advancement renders an irreversible trend that transforms all community enterprise into industries that can be evaluated by measuring their output.

Both Nader and Fuller suggest that output could be an even better thing than it is today. I cannot see what this would mean but that there would be even less "enough" of it.

I have shown that economists spell out the metaphysics on which contemporary men are willing to agree. Political parties have built on this seeming evidence the economists provide. They have become publicity firms for the same cornucopia and they compete for the right to use their banners and slogans to shove it down the throats of their clients. On a worldwide scale, capitalists and Communists share the crypto-

Stalinist fallacy. Major powers try to impose on each other their particular way of insuring minimum consumption levels for the masses. So powerfully has Stalinism corrupted our social imagination that we cannot conceive that an alternate institutional structure could be used in a technological society.

Our present technocopia is a society in which specialized producers monopolize the purpose of all major institutions, and growing productivity justifies their growing power. A political left, to be meaningful, would have to forego the various attempts to render our present institutions viable. It would have to focus on the task of inverting their trends towards rising productivity, which renders conviviality dysfunctional. A hospital now has the purpose of providing the sick with professional and paraprofessional services and of excluding any relative, friend or child who might want to care for and about a sick neighbor. Tolerable institutions would be those in which the productive and the convivial purpose temper each other. In such health centers a sick person having a neighbor would be well cared for at home. The health center would help the concerned friend to find the tools to care for the sick person and perhaps provide someone to show him how to use these tools.

Our present institutions are high-pressure production funnels that, by their very structure, contribute to the proliferation of increasing levels of subordinate professions and paraprofessions. Desirable institutions would by their very structure make it incumbent upon their managers to enable nonspecialists to teach, to heal, to move or to house each other in the hope that people who have been engaged in any of these specialized activities will initiate others into the role still provisionally in the hand of a specialist.

For example, such institutions might well preclude certain types of brain surgery. At a recent meeting I overheard a group of neurosurgeons make a surprising statement. They agreed that most of the special techniques that could contribute to healing, and for which operating rooms could in fairness be provided in Latin America, could be taught to a responsible peasant girl with a steady hand and intelligence in a matter of months. I repeated this statement to a group that included another doctor, a psychiatrist and a neurosurgeon.

The last-mentioned contradicted his colleagues, called them irresponsible. For the time being, I accepted his correction. But later in the evening, this same man privately explained to me why some neurosurgeons make irresponsible statements. He said that his was a frequently frustrating profession, that sometimes looking back on a week's work of multi-hour operations, one had to admit that practically all his patients had died, and of those who survived the intervention, few would be able to live everyday lives. We parted as friends, he agreeing with me that at least in Latin America, and for the moment, medical resources could well be spent in an alternate and better way.

Convivial institutions, providing tools that nonspecialists can learn to use when the need for them arises, inevitably impose limits on the tools that fit this purpose. It is quite easy to paint a scenario of alternate toolkits that would fit most of the needs of countries in which the majority of people needing tonsillectomies, bone settings or appendectomies cannot now get them. It is less easy to make restrictions on the medical toolkit plausible to citizens of countries where people have access to high technology. One reason for this difficulty is that most people are not aware of the cost they now pay in health-destruction in order to be allowed the high levels of health-service intake that they "enjoy."

On this point it is significant that a large percentage of new medicines that came into the United States market in the period between 1945 and 1970 were withdrawn from the market when the seventeen year patent protection had run out, and it ceased to be in the interest of the manufacturer to push the product. Some might have been withdrawn because the manufacturer wanted to push a new, more expensive product, for which he could again claim mysterious qualities and a monopoly over another seventeen year period. But much more frequently the item is withdrawn because, at best, it has not proven superior to a centuries-old generic, and, at worst, its side-effects were now amply documented and rendered further sales impossible. If Americans, Germans and Frenchmen understood that they do serve as human guinea pigs for extended testing of medicines that are still too expensive for the majority of poor people in the tropics, they might awaken to the advantages the limitation on the pharmacopoeia might mean for them.

In its present production-oriented structure, medical care translates into longer survival for a few notwithstanding a biosphere that is corrupted by doctors, geneticists and the factories that produce medical supplies. And for the majority of people in rich countries, such medical care serves the same purpose as coca does in Bolivia where the mine-owners use it in lieu of salaries: as a drug that keeps the Indian going deeper down into the pits, happily unaware of his hunger.

The present structure of medical institutions is built on the concept of indefinite backup and referral, by which both economic and human costs are escalated out of sight. Most alternate schemes for the delivery of medical services are nothing but rearrangements of backup agencies. Some want neighborhood health-centers in which paraprofessionals can set bones or other arrangements by which laymen can do it, but all want a hierarchy of places to which a sick man can be transferred (with or without the company of an advocate from his neighborhood) so that nothing that science considers feasible for his sake might be left undone. There is no way to insure a reorganized health-care system against being as impersonal as what we have, even though under a new name.

That limits must be set on the amount of medical services available per capita is clear, if for no other reason than not to impose the duty on the doctor of determining in each case when the patient is allowed to die. How such limits are to be set, and how the measurement of the height of the ceiling ought to be achieved is less clear.

SPEED: AN ILLUSTRATION OF LIMIT SETTING

How one could reach political agreement on an upper limit can be more easily illustrated in the case of the speed at which a society agrees locomotion of person is fast enough, not only for commuters but equally for ambulances, policemen and campaigning politicians as well.

At present the search for open-ended speed has made of vehicles a second type of luxury home for a minority. As I have indicated, this same open-endedness of speed forces the majority of people in a "mobile" society to switch from fixed to moving cages several times each day. In this process, the act of "dwelling" has become a luxury.

It ought to be possible to determine a level of speed at which most people compelled to use vehicles will spend less time in movement (which is something different from cruising), while depletion, pollution and destruction of health are kept to a minimum. The search for such a level has to start from insight into the present structure of transportation. The time spent moving, as I have shown, increases with the consumption of speed by a society, while, at the same time, locomotion between two points, both of which are desirable, becomes the privilege of fewer and fewer people. Commitment to more speed blinds us to the obvious. Such escalation only further increases time spent commuting at rising levels of pollution, depletion and unhealthy living.

The optimum level of speed would be a compromise between minimum time spent daily moving between equally attractive homes and work places at minimum levels of pollution with the maximum choice at minimum personal cost, and abstention from the use of mechanical transportation altogether. A truly radical political platform that presents voters with a well reasoned choice among possible profiles of upper limits for consumption should certainly contain such a speed limit.

The first reaction I get, when discussing this matter with people who, in principle, follow my argument, is that such an upper limit would have to be developed by experts. I doubt that this is true. Some very simple considerations will show that this speed limit within metropolitan areas would be somewhere in the order of 15 or 20 miles per hour. If people living in any of the major United States metropolitan areas were guaranteed effective locomotion permitting them to cover 15 miles in any given hour from any point to any point, they would be moving faster and better than they are now. We know that this could be achieved by banning private cars from the streets of New York, and that the saving in taxes that could result would make it possible for the city to provide transportation at minimum prices.

The setting of upper limits on certain dimensions is not only necessary (as in the case of medical services) and can be discussed in quantitative terms (as I have shown in the case of speeds of locomotion), it is also the only way of providing the majority with what they need to survive.

My proposal of a radical new politics setting an upper limit to consumption is not simply neo-Luddite. I do not propose the diminution in numbers or quality of the tools of life. What I do propose is a radical reevaluation of the part they and their production are to play in society and the individual's social life.

A society that sets lower limits to the goods and services to be provided to its members (whether in terms of quality or quantity) does not thereby contribute to the conviviality of their lives. In education, in health, in transportation, the intensification of the efficiency of the tool has in fact radically reduced the individual's freedom to use it in his own way, or even for his own purpose.

A politics of upper limits would supply to the individual a maximum power to determine what tools were adapted to his life, to produce and use them in his own way and for his own purpose in the service of his own life and that of others. A radical new politics would be a politics of conviviality.

ETHICAL AND MORAL ASPECTS OF GENETIC KNOWLEDGE AND COUNSELING

robert murray

——————————— ROBERT MURRAY ———————————

Robert Murray brought very valuable input to the Conference. As a medical geneticist and practicing physician he represented the intense concerns of genetic knowledge and technology in the context of clinical medicine. As a black man he reminded us of our too easy reliance on the technical solution, on human wisdom in diagnosing and treating problems, of the ethnic overtones of many of our noble schemes. He pleaded for a confidence in the wisdom of nature and the common man. He highlighted the elements of faith and humility that might direct our technological future more humanely.

INTRODUCTION

My approach to analyzing how ethics might influence genetic screening and counseling will be a relatively simple one. I shall try to look at part of the screening and counseling process from different points of view and compare the good things with the harmful things that can happen depending on what the physician says or does. I shall do this by trying to see how different aspects of screening and counseling affect major ethical values. These values are freedom, justice, security, well-being, truth telling and general welfare or general good of all patients, parents and the population. This is obviously not an exhaustive list of possible ethical values but the ones that seem important to me. Perhaps this exercise might be looked upon as the feeble efforts of a scientist to measure the unscientific.

THE PHYSICIAN AND THE INDIVIDUAL

The cornerstone of medical practice has been the doctor-patient relationship. Modern medical practice continues to emphasize the physician's responsibility to each individual patient. He must not only treat the patient's ills but, further, he must do no harm.

> I will follow that system of regimen which according to my ability and judgment, I consider for the benefit of my patients, and abstain from whatever is deleterious and mischievous.
> (Part of the Hippocratic Oath)

There are occasions when in the guise of abstaining "from whatever is deleterious and mischievous" the physician may withhold information or treatment that he judges would do more psychological harm if the patient were to learn about it. But always at the center of the clinician's concern is the individual; that particular patient with whom he is immediately involved. His interests, in the past, have usually extended beyond the individual only when communicable infectious diseases or toxic environmental agents have been involved, which might constitute immediate danger to members of the larger community.

Large scale screening for genetic disorders is another situation in which the focus of attention for the doctor has extended beyond the individual to the group. The group may be the family, a community or all of mankind. The difference here is that the conditions that concern the physician are not communicable or immediately dangerous but rather are dangerous in a futuristic sense. Furthermore, only a minority and in many cases a small minority of the total population is likely to be involved. The threat to the group as a whole is nebulous and vague compared to the threat of death from a communicable disease. But just as the emphasis in working with the community in communicable disorders is on prevention, the emphasis in screening for genetic disorders is not on treatment of disease, but prevention of the potentially diseased individual.

In the past doctors have thought of preventing disease in a positive sense; that is, by treating the living patient or his surroundings in a specific manner rather than by eliminating him. Smallpox, for example, has been prevented by giving people vaccinations so that contact with the infectious virus does not cause disease. Mental retardation that will almost always occur in diseases like phenylketonuria (PKU) or galactosemia is prevented by removing a particular amino acid, phenylalanine, in the first case, and the milk sugar, galactose, in the second case, from the diet of infants who have the specific mutations that produce these metabolic errors. The ability to prevent and possibly treat the disease, in this latter sense, has excited intense interest and has led to the development of massive programs of screening the population for diseases that are presumably caused by mutant genes or other errors in the genetic material. The dream of the doctor is, after all, preventing diseases from developing rather than curing them after they have been diagnosed.

THE DOCTOR'S DILEMMA

What could be better than to check all newborn infants at birth for as many known biochemical and chromosomal defects as possible? One would not only identify those babies who are diseased, but, better still, one would be able to assure the parents of those who are not affected that they need not worry about those conditions that have been tested for. And last but not least, the parents would be told what kind of treatment is available for those conditions that are discovered.

Herein lies a part of the clinician's dilemma. In most cases where genetic disease (or the potential for disease) is detected there is no effective therapy for the patient. If the chances for the patient's survival are very poor and death rapidly results from the disease, the fact that there isn't treatment may not appear to be oppressive. But if the condition is a chronic, debilitating, slowly progressive disease, such as particular muscular dystrophies or sickle cell disease, and there is no effective therapy available, knowing about the inherited condition before there are signs and symptoms of the disease may provoke increased patient or parental anxiety without offering any positive reassurance. There will be little benefit to the patient and possibly some degree of harm to the parents and patient, depending upon their emotional stability.

It might be argued that informing parents or patients of the genetic defect before there are signs and symptoms of overt disease infringes upon their feelings of security and well-being and in one sense the freedom of the parents and the patient. For although prior knowledge of the defect supports the ethical value, truth-telling, it does so at the expense of these three important values.

THE VALUE OF KNOWLEDGE

To the physician, as with other scientists and scholars, knowledge is in and of itself a value. This is a purist's point of view. The utilitarian, and many of today's youth ask of knowledge, "What good is it?" This is a valid question asked by many parents.

Some two or three years ago we briefly saw in our Heredity Clinic a four- or five-year-old Caucasian girl who had odd pigmentation of her skin and hair. We asked her to return to the clinic for more detailed diagnostic study, but her mother refused to bring her back again. In trying to persuade her to return to our clinic we told her that we wished to know for sure what her daughter's skin disorder was. Her mother replied, "If you can't cure my daughter or make her skin normal, what is the good of knowing? It may help you, but not me or her." For many parents knowledge of a potential problem disturbs their well-being without providing any practical benefits. Knowing ahead of time without some way of altering the course of the disorder is, to them, more an academic exercise than a benefit. Knowing, in this instance, interferes with the pleasure and sense of well-being that parents might have at least until such time as the first signs or symptoms of the particular disorder appear. In cases like this, ignorance can be bliss!

There is one special aspect of genetic counseling of particular importance. For while the physician takes away from the present well-being of parents by informing them of their child's condition he can help their future well-being by reassuring them of their innocence in the causation of the condition. He can make it clear that the disorder was a consequence of fate and help them to appreciate what they can do to help their child even if there is no effective treatment for the condition. He can help them to look at their child as a human being to be helped, not pitied. And he may be able to help them avoid or deal with self-pity in a positive manner.

The fact that most hereditary disorders now detected by screening have no effective medical therapy has been responsible for the current emphasis on intrauterine diagnosis followed by therapeutic abortion. The therapy in this instance is for the mother and father and not the embryo, which is eliminated because it is thought to be diseased. Furthermore this lack of possible treatment has pointed up how important it is to identify normal carriers of mutant genes, more specifically those genes that are recessives, so that individuals with genetic disease might not be conceived. Let us look at some ethical values in this screening and counseling of diseased or potentially diseased individuals.

ETHICS AND SCREENING FOR GENETIC DISEASE

In those states where screening for phenylketonuria (PKU) is required by law, there is an infringement on the freedom of choice and right to privacy of a given individual. But this abridgment of freedom can be justified because the security, well-being and quality of life of the child found to have this condition will be improved by the early detection of too much phenylalanine in the blood. The child can be placed on a corrective diet, low in phenylalanine, and thereby avert the retarded mental development that almost invariably results without this kind of treatment. The measures taken to ensure normal mental development are well worth those rights infringed upon.

There is another consequence of screening programs where there is detection and treatment of this and other hereditary

conditions. The usual fate of the mentally retarded PKU patient is social isolation in one way or another. These persons
are kept at home or in institutions where they don't have social contact with others. The net effect of this is that he or she
is unlikely to reproduce and the mutant genes they carry are
not passed on to the next generation. The effect of treating the
ˑKU patient is to significantly increase the chance that he or
she will marry and that the mutant genes carried will be
passed on to children and become part of the gene pool of the
next generation. The effect of this aspect of the screening program, called by some scientists negative eugenics, is to influence in a "negative" way the future quality of the human
gene pool. This means that the number of detrimental hereditary traits is increased. There is in the minds of most
physicians little question but that the human benefits—the
benefits of health, happiness and increased well-being—that
accrue to those children identified in this process far outweigh
any danger to the genetic makeup of mankind. Such danger is
questionable, or at least very long range, and it is possible that
scientific solutions may be found for this problem.

Screening for hereditary disease is, then, a mixed blessing.
Where specific treatment exists for the disease, the ethical
benefits far outweigh the medical risks and ethical detriments
that result. Where there is no therapy it may be that the emotional burdens imposed by prior knowledge may not be worth
the anxiety that can interfere with the chance of at least a
brief period during which parents can enjoy a positive sense
of well-being with the child. The physician may on one hand
exert a negative influence in the course of bringing truth to
the parents, but on the other hand, he can bring positive
benefits through effective genetic and medical counseling.

THE DILEMMA OF THE CARRIER

If specific, effective therapy is lacking for most hereditary
metabolic and chromosomal disorders, and if the destruction
of a diseased fetus places an almost insoluble moral burden on
the physician, there is still an alternative open to those determined to "prevent" genetic disease. Wherever possible, programs can be directed toward screening the population to fer-

ret out the normal heterozygous carriers of hereditary biochemical abnormalities. Heterozygous carriers have one normal and one abnormal gene for a particular trait. What would make an acceptable screening procedure would be:

1. A relatively simple, easily reproducible and reliable biochemical test.
2. That the human material required for testing be easily obtained and stable (blood, urine).
3. That, if anything, there should be no false negative tests for the carrier status.

If carriers for recessively inherited traits such as cystic fibrosis (5 percent of the population) and the blood disease, sickle cell anemia, are detected and told that they are carriers and counseled as to the significance of their state, genetically speaking, their freedom of mating and their well-being will be reduced at the expense of knowing. Through the information they have been given, particularly if they take positive action on it, their options for marriage will be reduced to varying degrees, depending upon the trait they carry. For example, in the United States, one in ten black men will be eliminated as a mate for a black female carrier of sickle cell trait (SCT) since she should consciously avoid marrying a man who also carries SCT if she wishes to eliminate the possibility of giving birth to a child with sickle cell anemia. Possible mates carrying other less common hereditary blood diseases are also eliminated since their children who have two different mutant genes for particular conditions will also be seriously ill. (The state of well-being of SCT carriers is also threatened by the possibly false information being disseminated that they might have a greater susceptibility to disease than non-carriers. The information currently available on this question is contradictory and a statement like this is unjustified.)

By the same token those subjects who are identified as non-carriers of *known* hereditary traits (i.e. recessively inherited traits) will have their state of well-being enhanced, their freedom relatively increased and their faith in science vindicated since they have received genetic "good news"!

What options are open to the individual now identified as a carrier?

1. The carrier might inquire of all prospective mates (either when dating or when introduced to each other) whether or not they are carriers for the same condition. It is clear that unless this sort of thing became accepted social behavior it might tend to squelch social relationships.

2. The carrier could marry, then check to see whether his or her spouse was a carrier. (Since one out of ten blacks is a carrier of SCT, the chances are nine in ten that a carrier will marry a non-carrier.) The problem here is that once two carriers have married they must either: a. not have children of their own; b. be able to detect the potential disease condition in early pregnancy (in the first trimester of pregnancy) in order to prevent the birth of a diseased child through therapeutic abortion if they do not wish to risk having an affected infant; c. or if the condition can be treated they need only worry about the exorbitant costs of modern medical care.

In the best of all possible worlds the carrier status of everyone for all mutant genes would be known. All of us carry not one but several mutant genes and so there would be no stigma attached to being identified as a carrier of a mutant or abnormal gene. Part of the mating process might consist of men and women comparing notes to find out who carried the same mutant genes. As knowledge of detecting the carriers of mutant or abnormal genes became more sophisticated, options for mating would be further and further restricted if people were to avoid marrying someone carrying the same mutations. It might be necessary to develop a computer matching service to help people find suitable mates. As yet only a small minority of mutant carrier states are known and fewer can actually be identified before the fact of the birth of an abnormal child.

It is in one sense, then, unfortunate that only certain carriers can be detected, for all those other individuals who are carriers and don't know it are deprived of the knowledge that might allow them to attempt to ensure the birth of normal offspring. On the other hand, it is unjust that carriers of hereditary traits be stigmatized or considered abnormal or inferior because we don't yet know how to detect most mutant genes in carriers.

PREVENTING GENETIC DISEASE BY KILLING

Mutant genes responsible for a number of illnesses are not only often present and functioning at birth, but can and often do produce their effects while the infant is still developing in the uterus. A small number of these genetic defects[1,2] can be detected in cells taken from the 12-20 week embryo and the disease "prevented" by aborting the embryo; in reality preventing the birth of the potentially diseased individual. There appears to be general medical acceptance of this approach to disease control but some strongly oppose it for it violates the physician's charge ". . . to give no deadly medicine to anyone if asked, nor suggest such counsel; and in like manner I will not give to a woman a pessary to produce abortion." (Part of Hippocratic Oath) The physician then, in preventing parental suffering by preventing birth, at the same time violates his ancient charge to preserve and maintain life. Technological advance has helped transform a savior of life into a destroyer of life, albeit of perhaps a reduced quality.

The physician on the one hand threatens the security and survival of the abnormal human embryo or fetus while on the other hand he enhances the well-being and freedom of the parents of the potential child. He trades off the good of the child for the good of the parents. But which is the greater good? In medicine the survival of the already born has usually been given greater weight than that of the not yet born. The unborn child has usually been sacrificed when the survival and well-being of the mother was threatened. Is the emotional security and well-being of the mother less important than her survival? It is on this basis that the majority of therapeutic abortions have been and are being justified.

Where there is specific medical treatment available it is possible to directly attack a specific condition, much in the way that Tay-Sachs disease (a type of idiocy) is being attacked by Kaback in a Baltimore Jewish population. The program is designed to solicit voluntary screening of large numbers of persons of Jewish ancestry for carriers of this condition. When couples who are both carriers are identified, each pregnancy can be checked and the embryos who are homozygous for the mutant gene can be detected by intrauterine diagnosis using cells taken from the amniotic fluid (the fluid that immediately surrounds the baby) and eliminated by therapeutic abortion. Although faced with a moral dilemma relating to abortion, the doctor might find himself under less restraint since the life expectancy of the usual Tay-Sachs patient is only two to four years. This kind of program has been justified because it costs less than allowing children with Tay-Sachs disease to be born and cared for in institutions until their death. Motulsky *et al* [3] have examined the pattern of premarital diagnosis that would be required to prevent births of children with different biochemically determined conditions, assuming that each couple will have two healthy children. It is clear from their analysis that the prevention of rare metabolic diseases (i.e. PKU and galactosemia) is much more expensive than programs to prevent more common conditions like sickle cell anemia and cystic fibrosis. But is it ethically justified to make decisions about health care purely on the basis of monetary determinations?

One can look at some kinds of preventive programs involving abortion as a kind of triage (an accepted medical practice in time of disaster). The idea is that time, money and effort should be expended on those individuals who are likely to benefit from them and so to survive. Other individuals are neglected. Although there is no clear-cut disaster evident, one can look at the justification for programs of preventive abortion through cost accounting as supporting triage of a sort, only instead of exercising "benign-neglect" of the affected individuals they are directly eliminated. The money that would have been spent in their treatment and support is supposed then to be available for the diagnosis and therapy of other conditions. There is no evidence that this is actually the case.

On the other hand, supposing it were possible to cure and make normal the individuals with these kinds of inherited diseases by spending large sums of money. Would there be the same support for these programs?

I would suggest that decisions relating to the preservation or destruction of human life should not be based on the same factors one would use in buying or selling property or making business deals. Cost estimate analysis might be the basis used for convincing foundations or government agencies to provide support for new programs, but *not* for determining whether or not a particular course of medical action ought to be taken. The ethical and moral implications of such actions are far too profound. Unfortunately, too many important medical decisions have been made and continue to be made mainly on a financial basis.

MASS SCREENING PROGRAMS FOR CARRIERS

Among the questions that must be answered before effective screening programs are instituted are: Who is to be tested? Should testing be voluntary or compulsory? What should be done with the information that is gotten from testing?

At first glance it would seem logical that testing should be done only in groups of people where the number of possible carriers of a particular genetic trait is fairly high. Only persons of Jewish ancestry would be tested for the carrier state for a particular type of disorder like Tay-Sachs disease while only blacks would be tested for sickle cell trait. If testing is voluntary and if there are no problems in identifying these groups, this might be an ethically acceptable approach to screening. But if testing for traits like these is made compulsory, especially in elementary schools, it might happen that children identified as carriers would be stigmatized as different, as being undesirable parents or as being weaker or less fit. A recent advertisement in *Ebony* magazine (October, 1971), for the purpose of raising money for sickle cell research, characterized carriers of sickle cell trait as being weak and requiring regular visits to their physicians as if they had some chronic disease condition. This kind of misinformation only helps promote the kind of stigmatization that might occur. If there is to be compulsory testing for traits like Tay-Sachs disease or sickle cell trait *everyone* should be tested since some Caucasian individuals of Mediterranean descent will also carry the sickle cell trait. It would also help to avoid further discrimination and separation of racial groups. Large scale screening programs must be allied with extensive educational programs to avoid the misinformation and "negative" labeling of carriers of hereditary traits that might result and perhaps has already begun. People already think that the reports of death associated with violent exercise in people with sickle cell trait means that children with sickle cell trait should have their physical activity limited.[4]

The information from screening is, of course, transmitted to the individual tested or his parents, depending upon his age. But it is not enough to report that the screening test is positive or negative. The patient must be educated about the meaning of the carrier state from a medical and genetic point of view. He should be instructed about the disease and the range of severity that occurs in the homozygous state. He must understand the condition well enough to make an intelligent or informed decision based on the information he has been given. If this is to be the *patient's* decision (and I believe it should be), the physician or counselor must be careful not to directly influence the patient's decision unless he has a very good reason to do so, and he can justify that to do so is in the patient's best interest.

It has been suggested that the information gotten from screening might be put into large central computers. This would allow periodic comparisons to be made and furthermore, the information would be available, with the patient's permission, to physicians in other parts of the country. This might seem a good idea on the surface but the problems of maintaining privacy of information stored in the computer and the absence of a foolproof method of safeguarding the patient's medical record are good reasons for postponing this move.

THE RIGHT NOT TO KNOW

Communications technology has made information almost instantly available to everyone in industrial societies. With this instant communication has come a strong emphasis and even insistence on the right to know. Information of all kinds is being made available to everyone. Medical information is no exception to this rule.

It seems to me that individuals also have a right not to know, if they consider it to be in their own best interest. If I don't know that my wife and I are carriers of a particular autosomal recessive trait then we are free to go ahead and conceive our own natural children. We might be lucky and have our first two or three children be normal. If on the other hand we have learned through a screening program that we are carriers of some particular genetic trait, we would have our freedom of reproduction compromised by such knowledge. In this case a couple has a greater degree of freedom through ignorance, and a better state of mind.

Those people who know they are carriers have a right to know who else is also a carrier so that they might take this information into account when making the choice of a mate. When faced with someone who does not know, and does not wish to know, the decision would be difficult.

Doesn't the couple who are both carriers have some obligation to society not to produce a child that will automatically be a drain on society's resources? On the other hand their right to have a child, even an abnormal one, should take precedence over their obligation to society. Through no fault of their own, their freedom, justice and well-being would be abridged in the guise of furthering the general welfare of society. The primary financial cost to society of supporting an abnormal individual is, in my estimation, far outweighed by the ethical and moral cost to the couple denied a child. One might just as well (as some have advocated and some states have attempted to legislate) deny the birthright to some couples because they are poor. This kind of denial cannot be justified at this time on a purely eugenic basis. Those who support society's right to maximize its quality must demonstrate to the satisfaction of many scientists what they mean by this and exactly how this can be accomplished.

I should like to illustrate the kinds of conflicts that might arise from the screening process by briefly reviewing three actual cases. The solutions offered in each situation may not be considered ideal by everyone, but seemed appropriate at the time they were considered. All the cases involved detection of the sickle cell trait.

Case 1—The husband of a childless, young black couple in their twenties was seen for genetic counseling because he learned that both he and his wife carried the sickle cell trait. The husband said that his wife, who wanted very much to have her own natural child, learned that she carried the trait during a medical workup for mild anemia. The husband, on the advice of their physician, had himself checked and learned that he was also positive for sickling. He learned something about sickle cell disease by reading, but he and his wife were discouraged because they were under the impression that sickle cell disease was a horrible, universally fatal disease about which nothing could be done. It was clear that they badly wanted their own natural children. After a thorough discussion of sickle cell anemia, the origin and significance of the sickle cell gene and what the genetic possibilities were, we discussed his feelings about the condition, and what decision he thought he might make. He said that he wanted to talk to his wife since he wasn't as discouraged as when he had arrived, especially since I pointed out that sickle cell anemic children aren't deformed or mentally retarded. I also brought him information about the accelerated studies on new therapies for sickle cell crises. He felt that he might be willing to try for one "natural" child if his wife agreed and that whether it had sickle cell anemia or not they would quit and adopt other children.

By presenting a totally negative picture to couples who both have sickle cell trait, the physician-counselor is preventing the birth of sickle cell anemic children but he is also denying couples the benefits and joys of their own natural children and perhaps keeping out of the reproductive gene pool "beneficial" genes that they might contribute.

Case 2—A 27-year-old black female brought her year old infant to the hospital because of anemia and poor physical and mental development. The child was found to have sickle cell anemia in the course of the medical evaluation of his anemia. Sickling tests were done on the mother and the putative father, the woman's common law husband. The mother's test was positive but the father's test negative. She was told that the father's test showed that he could not be the father of the child. The mother insisted that her common law husband *had* to be the child's father and she swore this "on her mother's grave." This is one of the strongest oaths that can be sworn by blacks from some communities and rather than dismiss this as just "another case of non-paternity" hemoglobin electrophoresis was performed. It was found that the common law husband's red blood cells contained only 5 percent of the hemoglobin as sickle cell rather than the 20 to 45 percent that is usually found in the red cells of subjects with SCT. The 5 percent of hemoglobin present was insufficient to produce sickling of red blood cells in the special sickling test.

The physician in this case might have produced familial discord *and* given incorrect counseling if he hadn't heeded the mother's insistence and performed more careful studies. This case further illustrates the kinds of serious errors that can occur when a screening test that can have false negative results is used. All screening for SCT should ideally be done by hemoglobin electrophoresis. The physician should be especially cautious in cases where non-paternity appears to be involved. Where there is a conflict between human relations (well-being) and scientific truth I have tended to sacrifice the truth to the well-being of the patient and the family as in this next instance. But cases like this are *rare* exceptions.

Case 3—A black couple was being interviewed to determine the psychological effects of sickle cell anemia on the development of their four-year-old child. The mother volunteered that she alone had the sickle cell trait. It was clear from further discussion that they did not understand the genetics of sickle cell anemia. It seemed clear that a lucid explanation to them of the genetics would probably raise the question of non-paternity and cause serious disruption of what appeared to be a reasonably compatible family relationship. The situation was explained by stating that the sickle gene in the egg from the mother was fertilized by a sperm in which a spontaneous mutation had occurred. This is genetically possible but it was not pointed out to the couple that mutations were as rare as they truly are. They were not interested in further genetic counseling since they had already completed their family.

I have, on the one hand, discussed the need for the physician to broaden his perspective beyond considerations of the needs of the individual to the needs of the community and on the other hand pointed out that the direction of the larger society should not negate the ethical values of the individual.

It is on the one hand unjust that everyone cannot yet know his or her "mutant gene carrier status" and on the other unfair that those whose status can be determined may be stigmatized.

The current state of genetic knowledge is such that we cannot and should not use coercive methods either direct or indirect to insist that carrier couples should not have children in cases where intrauterine diagnosis is unavailable.

Basically, my view is that the decision to act on genetic information is an individual rather than a collective one since there is little historical evidence that any group of persons knows better than any other group of persons what is best for the totality of mankind. There is, unfortunately, no group without a vested interest in the direction of our social future.

The physician and the physician-scientist have been placed in a very sensitive position by some of the advances in genetic diagnosis. It is vital that they be constantly reminded that in spite of the relative superiority of their knowledge over that of their predecessors, their knowledge of the total genetic function of the human organism is still relatively small.

If it sounds as if I am suggesting that the counselor ought sometimes to counsel ignorance rather than reveal the total truth, then you understand correctly. Knowledge is *not* always good. The whole truth is *not* always the best thing for everybody but withholding truth is only *rarely* justified. Although our total knowledge is limited I believe we know more about the need for stable human relations than we do about the beneficial or detrimental effects of particular kinds of mutant genes. The admonition "to do no harm" might well continue to serve as a rule of thumb in our naive and fumbling attempts to apply, in a beneficial sense, the rapid advances occurring in our knowledge of human genetics.

Footnotes

Portions of this manuscript were presented at the Conference on Ethical Issues in Genetic Counseling and Use of Genetic Knowledge, October 10-14, 1971; Sponsored by the Fogarty International Center, National Institutes of Health.

1. Nadler, H. L.: Indications for Amniocentesis in the Early Pre-natal Detection of Genetic Disorders, *in.* ed. Bergsma, D., *Symposium on Intrauterine Diagnosis.* Birth Defects: Original Article Series 7: 5-9, 1971.

2. Nadler, H. L.: Present Status of the Prenatal Detection of Genetic Disorders. Position paper from the Conference on Genetic Disease Control, Washington, D.C. December 1970.

3. Motulsky, A. G., Fraser, G. R., and Felsenstein, J.: Public Health and Long-Term Genetic Implications of Intrauterine Diagnosis and Selective Abortion *in.* ed. Bergsma, D., *Symposium on Intra-uterine Diagnosis.* Birth Defects. Original Article Series 7: 22-31, 1971.

4. Jones, S. R., Binder, R. A., and Donowho, E. M., Jr.: Sudden Death in Sickle-Cell Trait. New England Journal of Medicine 282: 323-325, 1970.

TECHNOLOGY AND THE FUTURE OF HUMAN SEXUALITY

robert t. francoeur

ROBERT T. FRANCOEUR

The technological revolution has made its greatest impact on morality in the area of human sexuality. Contraceptive technologies have wrought a major transformation in our cultural values regarding sexual expression. The new perinatal and neonatal technologies offer many challenges for personal sexuality and for family life and societal life as well. Robert Francoeur, an experimental embryologist and theologian, is well qualified to discuss these issues. His analysis is tempered by his Teilhardian vision of the enduring sanctity and emerging meaning of human life. The options he outlines for the arrangements of man's sexual future vividly represent the possibility and responsibility of this human freedom.

TECHNOLOGY AND THE FUTURE
OF HUMAN SEXUALITY

There are some rather unique characteristics apparent in the sexual revolution that embrace and invest nearly every aspect of our lives. In other revolutions triggered by new technologies it was very difficult, if not impossible, to diagnose the patient's condition while the fever of change still afflicted society and culture. This is not the situation with our sexual revolution. For some unknown reason the basic characteristics and trends of our sexual revolution are already evident even to laymen outside the deliberate and scientific disciplines of sociology, anthropology and psychology.

One unique characteristic of our sexual revolution is its apocalyptic swiftness in reaching the average citizen in the Western world, if not around our globe. Other technological revolutions created their own cultures and modified human behavior along with society's structure. The discovery of fire, wheels, gunpowder, internal combustion and steam engines, automobiles, nuclear power and the space age, each caused revolutions in man's way of handling and dealing with the world and each had its impact on human life. They modified and perhaps even created new forms of family life and varied the factors of human relations. But they accomplished this *slowly, gradually, over a period of centuries,* and two or three generations experienced the change as it spread through the human network. The cultural impact of our reproductive and contraceptive technology appears to be near-instant revolution. While these technologies wait in scientific minds for implementation, they are having a deep impact on the average man in the street. No doubt this is because other technologies have touched only the periphery of man's life, and not the very nature of man and woman as sexual persons —our deepest images of ourselves as sexual persons and our most treasured and seemingly stable images of male/female relations, marriage and family, as our contraceptive and reproductive technology does. The sexual revolution affects every man and every woman.

The reason for this ubiquitous influence stems from the synergistic interplay of three basic factors, or vectors, if you like, three elements that appear discrete and distinct but in fact are closely interwoven. If we were dealing only with the technologies of contraception and reproduction, society would have many years, decades, perhaps even generations to accommodate its emotions and psychology to the new developments. If our recent discoveries and technologies of the contraceptive pill, the intrauterine and intra-vas devices, the mini-pills, vasectomy and other contraceptive hardware had occurred in an earlier age, they would have been spread over centuries.

Today they are piled up within two or three decades. And the same acceleration is even more evident in the second phase of this hardware revolution, in our reproductive technology that, within the space of two decades, has brought us into the realm of the fabricated man. We now have new ways of making babies: artificial insemination, embryo transplants and soon artificial wombs and even asexual modes of reproduction. Not only can we modify our reproductive patterns, control conception and select our offspring for sex and perhaps other traits, we will soon be able to make man in new images and forms if we decide to. And all this within a single generation.

Add to this the synergistic effect of a simultaneous socioeconomic revolution epitomized in the phrase "Women's Liberation." As Teilhard de Chardin repeatedly pointed out, this century is witnessing a critical threshold in the hominization of man, the emergence of women as human beings and as persons both in social and in economic terms. It took man at least two million years to move well along the path of hominization; now suddenly, within a century, women are catching up with men. Adam's rib is becoming a responsible adult human.

These two factors, our contraceptive-reproductive technologies and women's liberation, taken alone could be devastating, but add to them the simultaneous repercussions of our global tribe and you have the most serious revolution ever to hit mankind. In the past, when a revolutionary breakthrough occurred in one isolated town, it took years to pass by word of mouth and personal instruction to neighboring villages and nations. In many cases wars and national barriers coupled with primitive modes of travel defused the impact on society. Today, if an unknown surgeon in Houston performs a heart transplant, he is an instant celebrity worldwide. Lawyers in New York become upset about their legal concepts of death, and people everywhere watching the evening news on television are shocked and stunned by the latest development in the medical manipulation of human life. A nerve network of copper wire and satellite reflectors encircle our globe to reach not just the scientific community but every man.

This global network I am convinced is extremely important, and its impact so unique that I am compelled to offer a couple of illustrations to emphasize my point of synergism.

I am sure you are all aware of the writings of a very prominent sociologist, counselor and cultural commentator by the name of Ann Landers. I would like to use her syndicated column as my first piece of evidence. On September 11, 1970, when my book UTOPIAN MOTHERHOOD was published, Ann Landers *very prophetically* and totally independently carried a brief article in her column. Briefly and in paraphrase that article said: "Dear Ann, I am very much interested in your recent discussion of artificial insemination because I am facing a serious question with this in my marriage. My husband is sterile and he insists that we use his father's semen for artificial insemination. My father-in-law says he will not recognize our child as his legitimate heir unless we agree to this. I admire my father-in-law very much and do not really object because the insemination would be artificial. But I do have some reservations. Would you give me your go-ahead and blessing?" Signed: Luana. The response: "Dear Lu, Since you have no real objection, go ahead, but you do so without my blessing. Have you thought about the psychological consequences for your husband? It would be total self-emasculation for him to let his father inseminate his wife. And what kind of an egomaniac is your father-in-law? And besides, my dear, have you thought what it would be like to give birth to your own brother-in-law?"

Let me offer another bit of evidence for the instant impact of our sexual revolution. Harriet Van Horne, a national columnist, interviewed me about the same time for a syndicated column that appeared in the *New York Post*. The discussion of new trends in human reproduction left her "in the state of cultural shock," but the mention of the possibility of combining artificial insemination ("ethereal copulation" as it was termed in the nineteenth century) with frozen semen prompted a forty-year-old housewife in Poughkeepsie, New York, to drop me a note. The woman said she had four healthy children but she and her husband wanted to plan for one final child, and could I help them obtain some frozen semen from Nobel Laureate Linus Pauling.

Then, as a result of my appearances on several nationwide television shows, the editors of a motion picture magazine decided to twist together some gossip about Richard and Liz

Burton with my comments about the possibility of embryo transplants or artificial inovulation. "Ever since Liz married Richard she has had one wish: to carry his child. And now the miracle can happen. All Liz and Richard have to do is consult with Dr. Francoeur at Fairleigh Dickinson University and arrange for an embryo transplant to a surrogate mother. If Richard can give Liz a million dollar diamond he can easily have a surrogate mother to carry their baby and pay her union wages for nine months plus severance pay."

That kind of article irritates me, but it is a good illustration of how technological developments can reach people when they pick up an overly popular magazine.

Finally a classic illustration of the synergistic relation of reproductive technology and our instant global communication. The chairman of my department at Fairleigh Dickinson is a classical plant taxonomist who likes to razz me about my writing "science fiction." But this summer when he returned from vacation I found the opportunity to ask him about "science fiction" in his sleepy little country town of Bernardsville, about ten miles west of our campus.

The "science fiction" began when Paul Grossman, a fifty-two-year-old music teacher with tenure and fourteen years' experience in the Bernardsville elementary school, visited Dr. John Money at the Johns Hopkins University Hospital during the 1971 Easter vacation. Happily married and the father of three teenaged daughters, Paul Grossman returned to his teaching position, his wife and daughters, as a woman. Paul had become anatomically and in personality Paula, after a transsexual operation. Mrs. Paula Grossman informed the school board that she wanted to continue teaching music in the Bernardsville school. The subsequent meetings of the panicked school board were aired on nation-wide television, with Mrs. Paula Grossman, her wife, Mrs. Ruth Grossman and their three daughters sitting in the front row of the school auditorium during the hearings. In the end, the school board decided not to renew her tenured contract, and Paula's lawyer instituted court proceedings, claiming job discrimination on the basis of sex under the 1962 federal law.

I think it is sad and even disastrous that this reproductive revolution should suddenly, within a few years, break on the unsuspecting public. Granted the Victorian secrecy of our American culture, it was really unthinkable that we should openly face the gradual emergence of our contraceptive and reproductive technologies from the ivory-towers of science into the realm of everyday life. It was not until the openness of today's young people, the first generation to mature sexually in a contraceptive pill culture, forced the American public to face human sexuality-sensuality in the Woodstock image that we have been able to deal openly with the history of our contraceptive and reproductive technologies in the public and mass media.

Let me sketch that history very briefly, touching on our present capabilities and possible developments in the next decade or two.

Artificial insemination began two hundred years ago when Lazzaro Spalanzani, an Italian embryologist and priest, tried his hand at manipulating the mating of frogs and dogs. In 1799, in England, the first woman was artificially inseminated, and the technique of "ethereal copulation" found several proponents and advocates in American medical circles during and after the Civil War.

Artificial insemination, however, did not come into extensive use either in human medicine or animal husbandry until the late 1950's when some English scientists found that glycerol could protect semen perhaps indefinitely from the damaging effect of cold storage and freezing. In October of 1971 New York City received its first commercial frozen sperm bank for humans, an expansion of the fourteen-year-old Genetic Laboratories, Inc., of Minneapolis, Minnesota.

Embryo transplants are now also a reality, at least in part. For about two years scientists at Cambridge University have been working with some fifty childless wives. Each of these women has blocked fallopian tubes that prevent conception and pregnancy. The hope of Dr. Robert G. Edwards and Dr. Patrick C. Steptoe is that they can superovulate these women with hormone therapy, collect the eggs surgically for fertilization with the husband's semen in a test tube, and then after incubating the fertilized egg for several days in a special culture medium transplant the embryo back into the womb of the woman, thereby bypassing her blocked tubes and allowing her to become pregnant. But while this work has been proceeding, with a minimum of progress reports, Dr. Landrum B. Shettles achieved the first successful transplant of a human embryo from one woman to another at Columbia Presbyterian Hospital in New York City. Shettles' technique involved fertilizing the egg of a woman whose ovaries had been removed with semen from her husband and then implanting the resultant embryo in the womb of a woman scheduled for a hysterectomy several days later. The transplant has been successful and the embryo was developing normally when checked during the hysterectomy two days later.

Beyond the technique of embryo transplant is the fascinating "brave new world" of artificial wombs, being developed in a dozen forms in a dozen laboratories around the world. The most promising form of artificial womb is that being developed at the National Institute of Heart and Lung Diseases in Bethesda, Maryland, by Drs. Kolobow, Zapol and Vurek. There a ten gallon plexiglass fish tank with an artificial heart, lung and kidney attached is being tested with premature lamb fetuses in an attempt to save their flickering lives. In the attempt to learn more about the unknown processes of birth, this artificial womb has turned up some interesting and helpful information. For instance, what happens in the fetus just before birth to shift the blood supply from the umbilical cord into the lungs at just the right moment? Dr. Kolobow and others have found that the oxygen level in the blood is a critical factor in this shift, and have experimentally tested this hypothesis. In one case a lamb prematurely removed from its womb was placed in an artificial womb with its blood and nutrients flowing through the artificial lung (extracorporal membrane oxygenator), artificial heart and dialyzing kidney machine. When the oxygen level in the blood was shifted, the lamb developed a sucking reflex and was ready to be removed from the tank. Out of the womb with its artificial umbilical cord detached, the lamb led a normal life for some hours until the doctors changed the oxygen content of its blood and the circulation shifted from the lungs back to the umbilical circuit. Reintroduction into the artificial womb was followed some time later by a second removal or birth. The lamb ended up with a double birthday.

Personally I am very skeptical about the artificial womb being used for a full-term nine-month pregnancy. I think there are *so many factors* of proteins, hormones and enzymes involved in a natural pregnancy, essential to normal development, about which we know practically nothing, that the chances of producing a biological and/or psychological monster are inescapable. The artificial womb will be perfected in ten or fifteen years, but it will still have to be tested with human fetuses and what do we do with the inevitable mistakes? For premature babies I see no moral problem because we are accepting the risk in a last ditch effort to save a human life—whether this effort is necessary or not is another question. But for a full-term nine-month pregnancy, I do not think the advantages outweigh the disadvantages today.

Asexual reproduction is undoubtedly the most grotesque and enticing of our new reproductive techniques. Still in its primitive phases, cloning (producing a group of organisms, asexually, from a single common ancestor) will be with us within a decade or two if we accept the assurances and warnings of two Nobel Laureates in the field of genetics, Joshua Lederberg and James Watson.

Overly simplified but not distorted, cloning can be reduced to the following technique. A small piece of epithelial tissue will be removed from your arm and the individual microscopic cells are separated with special enzymes. Then using special culture media, now being developed, we will hopefully trigger those isolated cells back to their "undifferentiated embryonic" unspecialized genetic condition, and start them developing all over again, this time into a whole organism rather than a piece of skin. The result would be a dozen or a hundred of your identical twins, your xeroxed body minus a few years.

This brief sketch of our reproductive capabilities leaves many listeners with the impression of "the mad alchemist," the mad scientist in his ivory tower, the Frankenstein who wants to play God. This is a total distortion, however understandable when you realize that for most people these developments come as a total and stunning thunderbolt out of a serene blue sky. It is crucial in achieving an objective picture of our sexual revolution to appreciate the motivation and source of this reproductive technology. The motivation stems from two areas: first, the very practical and economically important area of animal husbandry—95 percent of all the cows in this country today are artificially inseminated with frozen semen making the bull almost obsolete; and second, the very human concern for the suffering of childless couples and of fertile women who want to limit their family size. I cannot emphasize too much the vital importance of these two motivations behind our reproductive technology. That some applications of this technology are morally or emotionally questionable stems not from the basic human motivation, but rather from the ambivalence of subsequent applications by men otherwise motivated.

Let me illustrate this briefly. Embryo transplants were first developed by veterinarians as an economical solution to the problems of increasing the production of prize calves and lambs. Adult animals shipped into a country must remain in quarantine for some time before being released. How much simpler to superovulate a ewe, artificially inseminate this prize mother with semen from a prize ram and then transfer the fertilized eggs to a surrogate rabbit womb. The rabbit can easily pass through customs and on to the veterinarians in some developing nation for retransplantation to fifty to one hundred surrogate ewe mothers. The result is a flock of fifty to one hundred prize lambs in the space of a single pregnancy period. The technique is 75 percent successful today. And as Dr. Steptoe in Cambridge asked when confronted by women with blocked fallopian tubes who were desperate to have a child of their own, "Wouldn't any doctor, any human think seriously about using the proven technique of embryo transplant to help these women?"

But then comes the question: just because we can help, should we? In New Jersey, a childless wife went to Columbia Presbyterian Hospital seeking a solution to her sterility. The doctors ovulated her with Clomid, an ovulant inducer, and she had a single child. The technique was repeated two years later, and again, though her body was sensitized to the drug and the chances of a multiple birth were high, she had a single birth. But then she tried a third time, and gave birth to quintuplets. This I am convinced is irresponsible medicine. I think she should have been allowed to have one child of her own with the aid of Clomid, perhaps even two, but certainly not a third try. Adoption should have been urged for that third child.

This illustration and the possibility of cloning and artificial wombs highlight some of the crucial questions scientists, embryologists and gynecologists are beginning to deal with. The social impact of these developments on human values is becoming more and more a topic of real concern for the scientific and medical communities, but to be handled properly and with full respect for human values, our base of discussion must include those very people who are most affected by this technology, the man and woman in the street, the layman.

Let me turn back to Paula Grossman and Ann Landers to illustrate a major problem in our apocalyptic age. One of the surest signs that we are moving into a new world, into a new culture, appears when our language breaks down. How do Paula's three teen-aged daughters refer to their "former father?" How do we verbalize the relationship between their mother Ruth and ————? Because this is apparently a happy marriage, we can ask what obligation the state might have to step in, to annul the marital bond or implicitly recognize the marriage of two females. Will the Internal Revenue Service allow them to continue filing a joint husband and wife tax return? And what about Luana giving birth, as Ann Landers suggested, to her own brother-in-law? What if the woman from Poughkeepsie wanted to use the frozen semen of her grandfather who had been dead for ten years? Is artificial insemination a violation of marital exclusivity and fidelity, is it adultery? It was declared adultery in one divorce case by a judge who then had to try to explain how the artificially inseminated wife and the female gynecologist could be guilty of adultery. If a single woman decides to perform an act of Christian charity and carry her married sister's child because her sister is prone to miscarriage, is she still a virgin after the embryo transplant?

In terms of our traditional language, puzzle out this involved case of parenthood: a Russian woman with non-functioning ovaries marries a sterile Australian aborigine. They decide not to adopt and ask for an ovarian transplant from a Nigerian woman who is willing to donate one of her ovaries. The transplant is successful and because the husband is sterile they use artificial insemination with the frozen semen of an Eskimo who died ten years ago and had outstanding heredity. Then because the woman is prone to miscarriage, an embryo transplant is performed using an Irish woman from the Bronx as a surrogate mother. The resultant child then has a genetic mother, a biological mother who carried it, and a social mother. Fatherhood is similarly compounded.

The problem of language leads us very directly into the more basic question of our traditional conception of *marital fidelity*. Traditionally we have viewed marital fidelity in terms of sexual exclusivity. In this context, some moral theologians have condemned artificial insemination as a violation of the sexual exclusivity of the married couple, even when the insemination is performed with full consent of both husband and wife. I find this judgment too restricted to the concept of marital fidelity in terms of "property rights." It presents the relationship between husband and wife in terms of property and then only by reducing marital intimacy to genital relations. There is a much more realistic and human perspective that does not take its inspiration from the pagan ethos of property and justice, but rather from the Christian perspective of fidelity as loyalty.

Let me pursue this point of intimacy. In common everyday usage we take the word intimacy in a Victorian overtone as a euphemism for sexual relations. This is hardly a proper perspective or equation if *human sexuality is coextensive with human personality*. If, as I maintain, human sexuality cannot be reduced to genitality, then everything we do is sexual because we are sexual persons. Then also the restriction of "intimacy" overtly or covertly to sexual relations is a total distortion and extremely dangerous in our handling of human relations. If everything we do is sexual, then I believe it is un-Christian to continue perverting our biblical conception of marital fidelity in three ways: first, it is un-Christian to reduce marital fidelity to genital exclusivity between a married couple; second, it is un-Christian to reduce our conception of human intimacy to sexual relations; and third, it is un-Christian to rule out sexual relations in the broad context between people not married to each other.

I would like to pursue intimacy as a key concept in the reproductive revolution in terms of the biblical concept of *yahda,* the blunt Hebraic, non-euphemistic term for sexual intercourse as a deep personal relationship between two humans. The question then becomes this: can *yahda* between sexual persons be limited to marriage? And if so, then how do we depersonalize and restrict male/female relations outside marriage? On any and all levels? As a concrete example I recall the reaction of one of our college girls when she read the manuscript for my book UTOPIAN MOTHERHOOD. She was very upset because of her own experience when I raised questions about marital fidelity. A very popular and charming young woman, she had many friends. Many of these had recently married and suddenly she found that her male friends were *forbidden territory.* She had been accustomed to occasionally sharing a Coke and her problems with them as other girls did with an older brother. Suddenly, now married, these same fellows had to be approached as impersonal couples. No longer could she relate to them as young males. Intimacy on anything but the most casual level was ruled out because of the equation between intimacy and sexual intercourse.

This crucial human question of intimacy has been explored recently and well dealt with from a Christian perspective by Rustum and Della Roy in their book HONEST SEX. Pursuing their insights I wonder whether in our marriage oriented society in which exclusivity and intimacy are reduced to sexual terms we have in effect created an unnecessary and abnormal fear of personal relations. I am more and more convinced that this is exactly what we have done. I think we have to begin asking the very serious question about fidelity: does marital fidelity, or any fidelity have anything essential to do with genital exclusivity? Or from a more historical and cultural viewpoint, has our concept of marital fidelity as sexual exclusivity developed as a necessary outgrowth of our patriarchal pastoral roots where the property rights of the husband over his wife and the father over his unwed daughter reign supreme? Or from a different angle, have we perhaps placed too heavy a burden, an impossible burden, on genital intercourse by claiming that in that act alone is the total gift possible between two people? Can sexual intercourse be the sole source of intimacy between people, and if we claim that it is with a married couple, are we not perhaps demanding too much of an isolated human act, however personal and symbolic it might be?

I wonder whether the theology of the Oneida Community in the last century might not be more truly Christian than our present understanding of intimacy. The Oneida Community claimed that monogamy was the ultimate apostasy of Christendom because it was restrictive and selfish. The Oneida Community believed in group marriage, that all the saints were married to each other, only parenthood being restricted. Today our reproductive technology has separated sexual intercourse and procreation. And this fact suggests that we ask whether Oneida might not have been prophetically anticipating the culture now being created by our reproductive technology. Intimacy, the younger generation cries out, is not "hot genital focused sex," it is rather "cool and diffused, low-keyed." Intimacy is oriented eschatologically towards the whole community.

These are the reasons why we must try to discern where our reproductive technology is leading us, what kind of culture it seems already to be creating within our society.

The vast majority of social commentators are reluctant to project any definite outlines for the future of male/female relations beyond the rather naive and traditional suggestion of Alvin Toffler and others that serial polygamy and extramarital relations will increase. Frankly, I find this overly timid and unnecessary when the trends are already quite evident in our society, provided we are willing to break out of the traditional safe deductionism of marital fidelity to genital exclusivity and provided we are willing to think creatively about the whole realm of intimacy and fidelity in terms of personal responsibilities and loyalties. The trend, as I project it, is toward the complete democratization of the alternate life styles heretofore restricted to the bohemian and aristocratic subcultures within our society. But the extension of this traditional pluralistic set of life styles is radicalized by the addition of some new options and more important by the new and more human conception of intimacy and fidelity touched on above.

Until recently men and women had to fit into some very elementary and simplistic pigeon-holes. For women there was the choice of the "fair white maiden," the "snow princess" of the movie CARNAL KNOWLEDGE, the shy, non-intellectual asexually pure mother-wife and the "dark lady." As a non-voluntary option there was the pathetic spinster, hovering on the fringes of a marital-oriented society. On the base of these classic stereotypes, men have for centuries built their own image of what it means to be masculine: the responsible father, the playboy bachelor and the open or covert wolf.

These stereotypes gave society a very stable and neat situation that endured for centuries until the advent of women's liberation, our contraceptive and reproductive technology and the pot-boiling ingredient of mass instant communications. Suddenly all the neat male/female stereotypes are fractured and our society is faced with a whole range of options, many of which are not new and in fact have a long and interesting history in Western culture. But in preserving our mythic monogamous image we have consistently ignored these venerable options because they made us uncomfortable in terms of our stereotypes. Now the subterranean options are emerging into the full light of day. Some of them, complemented by totally new options, contain, I believe, the paradigms of the next decade or two. Without risking the role of prophet, I still feel safe in highlighting a variety of such paradigms as offering the basis for male/female relations in the years ahead, provided these are viewed as flexible options, which the individual may select as attractive and viable at various stages of his or her life.

AN INVENTORY OF ALTERNATE PATTERNS
IN SEX, MARRIAGE AND PARENTHOOD

Obviously, some of the options listed below will prove more viable and attractive than others in terms of solving the tensions and problems we can expect to encounter tomorrow. Reading the signs of today's society offers more than enough evidence, I am convinced, to highlight seven alternate styles of male/female relations and to propose that these will be the most common and viable as we move into the pluralistic culture of tomorrow's global tribe.

1. A few years ago when Margaret Mead first proposed a trial, or two-step, marriage, many people became quite upset, even though this pattern has a venerable history in the Jewish custom of espousal and the European custom, common in both Protestant and Catholic communities, of "window courting." The only difference is that these earlier forms of trial marriage were aimed at ascertaining the fertility of the bride-to-be while modern trial marriages are serving a more human and personal function in terms of individual and mutual maturation.

The inadequacy of the term premarital, however, and even more so of the concept of trial marriage covering all the informal cohabitation of single people indicates that the "trial marriage" of coming years will differ radically from the Jewish espousal, window courting and Margaret Mead's two-step or trial marriage. The new model now emerging appears to be assuming lines similar to those proposed by Robert H. Rimmer in his popular novel, THE HARRAD EXPERIMENT, except that social structure and acceptance is still absent. Rimmer describes a socially accepted living environment for young people in which coed cohabitation and premarital sexual experiences are structured within an education framework. This educational structure focuses on making the young adults aware of mankind's groping and varied attempts to cope with human sexuality, love and parenthood over the ages. It would serve as a guide to human values so that the youth would not be left to their own devices as they are today. The present situation hardly promotes the fullest development of young people's potential as sexual persons; it seems almost deliberately engineered to make this maturation as painful and risky as possible. Maturation of our youth could be much easier and surer if we, society, were to establish a whole series of Harrad-like environments where young people of college and high school age could mature and adequately prepare for their lives in a pluralistic culture.

2. Serial polygamy or consecutive monogamy is already with us in our extensive divorce and remarriage customs. Alvin Toffler, author of FUTURE SHOCK, maintains that this will be the most common pattern with the majority of people

engaging in several trial marriages before moving into a parental marriage with another partner, and then into a maturity marriage with yet another partner before settling down in a retirement marriage perhaps with several females for each male. Given the adolescent "hot sex" romantic marriage image of most people and their fear of working out a new definition of fidelity, this serial polygamy pattern is likely to be the most common.

3. Flexible monogamy, I am convinced, will be the most functional and viable pattern in the years to come. This pattern retains the best elements of the traditional couple marriage in terms of stability and child care, and also adapts to the tensions of women's emergence in society, extended life expectancies, mobility and the need for variety in human intimacy on all levels. Thus a couple can look to and work for a life-long relationship as a practical ideal while adopting a concept of marital fidelity as commitment and loyalty. Comarital relations for both spouses would be accepted as complements and supports for the life-long relationship.

Here I would suggest the concept of satellite relations. A variety of satellite relations are possible within the context of a couple marriage: the brief but deep penetration of a comet into the couple's orbit, or more lasting intimate relations orbiting the couple at various levels. The satellite concept allows for various types of pair bonding: the equal relationship of twin stars, or the subsidiary relation of sun and moon among others. It also allows for the risk of personal collisions encountered in astronomy as well as in human relations. The satellite concept also maintains the primacy of the couple bond as central in the functioning of flexible monogamy.

In his most recent novel, THURSDAY, MY LOVE, Robert Rimmer describes a relationship that very closely illustrates what I term flexible monogamy and he labels synergamy, or an open-ended form of monogamy. The relationship he describes and advocates as the form most suitable to our present and future needs involves "structured adultery," a monogamous marriage in which the couple's comarital or satellite relations are socially accepted and confirmed by a religious commitment. Rimmer's terminology often clouds the issue by using the classical derogatory language of "adultery," "affair" and the like. He is in fact not describing the traditional cheating affair, but rather a new type of constructive, complementary relation. His argument is for a socially sanctioned marital structure in which both husband and wife are bound to each other in a life-long commitment that accepts the impossibility of either spouse satisfying all the complex polyhedra needs of the other and hence recognizes their mutual need for supplementary relationships of varying intensities for their continual growth together. In HONEST SEX, the Roys describe several such comarital relations that integrate third partners, usually for a period of from two to five years. After that period, it seems, the individuals change enough to suggest a shift in the plane of intimacy, and often a drift away from the comarital relation involving (genital) intimacy.

4. Triangular marriages, or bigamy, usually involving two women and one man rather than the reverse, will also be common. When John Cuber and Margaret Harroff, sociologists at Ohio State University, surveyed the life of middle-class and upper middle-class Americans in 1965, they found that not infrequently the most creative and productive people in the communities and churches were involved in triangle relationships, almost always based on two households. Within the past few years, from what I can gather from a number of sources, a new tendency is appearing with triangular relationships based on a single household. An interesting bitter-sweet anticipation was portrayed in François Truffaut's classic movie, JULES AND JIM; Rimmer offers a more typical version in THE REBELLION OF YALE MARRATT.

5. Polygamy for senior citizens has been recommended by geriatric specialist Victor Kassel and the United Presbyterian statement on sexuality as a solution to many pressing economic, social, health and psychological problems of older people who are now forced to live alone on insufficient income, isolated from their children, unable to share their problems in a common life. With the number of women over sixty fast approaching double that of men over sixty, communal life is already being explored in Florida and other retirement centers.

6. The single, non-celibate life will take on new dimensions as we continue to separate sexual intercourse from procreation and view sexual intercourse as a valid mode of interpersonal communion and communication not limited to married couples. This new awareness will greatly reduce the image of the single person as a potential threat to monogamy.

7. The last of the seven life styles that I believe will be dominant in our emerging pluralistic society is briefly encompassed under the general label of contractual marriages. One form of contract marriage, based on the single element of duration, has been considered by the state of Maryland. This would offer the young couple a choice between an "until death do us part" traditional marriage license and a "three year renewable contract" license.

It seems likely, given the ever accelerating pace of change and the growing complexities of life, that the traditional simplicity of an unchanging, life-long marriage contract will be replaced for many with flexible, individualized contracts drawn up to suit the needs and desires of the individual couples. These contracts will contain specified renewable terms and arrangements for amendments to be made as the need arises. Most of the contract terms will undoubtedly center on the responsibilities toward children, but others will deal with economic arrangements and agreed-on sharing or division of domestic chores and work outside the home. Contract details may also include specifications guiding decisions about where the household will be located and whether a better job offer for the wife would occasion a transfer of domicile. Other stipulations may be spelled out regarding comarital and satellite relationships.

Complementing, and at times overlapping these seven dominant life styles, will be thirteen other options in sex, marriage and parenthood.

8. Single parents. One in ten minors in this country are in the custody of a single parent, and the number increases each year as divorced parents are augmented by the growing number of unmarried women who decide to have and keep a child.

9. Retirement parenthood, or the postponement of parent-hood until an early retirement age. This is increasingly possible as commercial firms and union contracts allow for full retirement benefits after twenty years' employment. The Irish have been doing this for years for economic reasons.

10. We are likely to witness the emergence of specially trained couples who will assume the role of parents as their jobs.

11. The third or supplementary parent: single or married people who take a special interest in parenthood—the camp counselor, the school teacher, the Scout leader, the Big Sister or Big Brother, and others who complement and reinforce the efforts of the natural parents.

12. Multilateral relationships involving two or three couples are another paradigm we can expect to encounter with increasing frequency. In such relationships, four seems to be a fairly unstable number with four-party marriages often evolving into triangles, or expanding to five or six parties. Perhaps this is a carryover of Buckminster Fuller's geodesic dome principle into social relations, but it is evident that groups of five or six can better tolerate slight frictions that would create intolerable tensions in a four-party relationship.

13. Two single people of the same sex who find it convenient to live together in a modified family structure, sharing or dividing the traditional male/female roles.

14. The group or communal type of marriage, for which an interesting precedent exists in the Oneida Community.

For fifty years, from 1831 to 1881, John Humphrey Noyes directed the fascinating Oneida experience in upstate New York, an open-sexual community rooted in an ultra-fundamentalist Methodist tradition and involving at its peak over three hundred adults. Oneida's theology is very interesting in its eschatological dimension: Christ's death and resurrection has thrust all the saints on earth into the state of the Parousia (the Second Coming), and since Christ tells us that in this afterlife all the saints will love one another fully, the state of monogamy is both selfish and the grand apostasy of the Christian church. Oneida thus opted for what they called "complex marriage," a society in which everyone was married to everyone in the community. Sexual (amative) relations were permitted to all, but reproduction was restricted to couples approved by the community.

Oneida succeeded I believe because it combined a clear transcendental orientation, a highly disciplined structure, a charismatic leader and a strong technological affinity. Many of these characteristics are missing in today's communes, and this makes me very skeptical about their persistence outside the academic and professional realms.

15. The celibate marriage is also possible in this pluralistic culture. Two friends of mine in Minnesota have written a book, NEW DYNAMICS IN SEXUAL LOVE. Robert and Mary Joyce argue that a marriage can be co-creative, without expressing its love in sexual intercourse and without being procreative. Their eschatological projection is exactly the opposite of the Oneida Community, for they look forward to a "virginal universe" in the life hereafter for which their celibate marriage is a witness and preparation. I do not accept their eschatology, but I am convinced that their option has a definite witness in two areas. First, the life-long celibate marriage, while not common, can bear witness to the fact that most marriages can expect occasional periods of celibate love and intimacy for a variety of healthy reasons. Second, the life-long celibate marriage can witness to the reality and value of male/female intimacy which need not be expressed in sexual intercourse. For our sex-intercourse-orgasm obsessed culture these are valuable witnesses.

16. The celibate marriage will be complemented by those individuals who freely choose to remain single and celibate for life. This single life, allowing for male/female intimacy but excluding genital intercourse, will witness to the fact that male/female relations are possible on a deeply intimate basis without necessarily finding expression in sexual intercourse. This celibate life will also tend to reduce the marriage obsession of

today's culture that drives young people into marriage before they are ready for it, or when it is not their real vocation.

17. The gay or homosexual union is now being tested legally in several states where homosexuals are seeking the legal right to marry. This development has an economic as well as a social basis, and brings to the fore the consequences of our separation of sexual intercourse from procreation. In the past homosexuality has often been condemned as immoral because it was unnatural, meaning non-procreative.

18. Unstructured cohabitation (living together) will be accepted for many young people turned off by all institutions. Some theologians see this as a form of the ancient *matrimonium in fieri* and thus not entirely contradictory or unacceptable to traditional Christian theology.

19. In many relationships the husband and wife will reverse or alternate for a time the traditional roles of breadwinner/ house keeper. This may even be a permanent arrangement.

20. The traditional sexually exclusive life-long couple marriage, I am also convinced, will remain an attractive option, but only for a small minority. It is already in the minority if we take seriously the statistics on divorce and remarriage and on extramarital relations. Couples who choose this style will have to find solutions for the increasing tensions of mobility, the equalization of the sexes (women's liberation), and especially the dangers of isolation and monotony generated by an increasing life expectancy, which may reach a hundred or more years within this generation.

In closing this list of options at twenty I am not denying the possibility of some unmentioned paradigm emerging. As traditional stereotypes fade and we come to appreciate the uniqueness of the individual person as well as the fallacy of our mythic monogamous culture, new life styles will emerge as socially accepted options. In this context each individual will in fact be free to work out his or her own unique life pattern. This will likely involve more than one of the models listed above, and each individual will create his or her own unique combination and sequence of options, for what may be attractive to one person at one phase of personal growth may not be attractive or viable for that same person at another time, or for another person at any time.

Granted this pluralism, this open democratization of heretofore restricted behavior, what kind of human and Christian values should we be concerned with in this variety of human relations? There is certainly a wide diversity in the advantages and disadvantages, problems and benefits to be derived by different people in the various models of life and relations. But even more fundamental, and transcending the inappropriateness of legal black-and-white pigeon-hole morality, is a basic set of human and Christian values that can be applied to all the paradigms cited above.

Nowhere have I found these basic values of human relations more concisely and beautifully stated than in the task force document issued by the United Presbyterian Church:

> We regard as contrary to the covenant [of Jesus] all those actions which destroy community and cause persons to lose hope, to erode their practical confidence in the providence of God, and to lose respect for their own integrity as persons. Clearly, such actions are not susceptible of being catalogued, for sexual gestures which may in one instance cause deep guilt and shame, whether warranted or not, may in another context be vehicles of celebrating a joyous and creative communion between persons.
>
> By the same token, those sexual expressions which build up communion between persons, establish a hopeful outlook on the future, minister in a healing way to the fears, hurts and anxieties of persons and confirm to them the fact that they are truly loved, are actions which can confirm the covenant Jesus announced.

Then, after highlighting the "Christian calling to glorify God by the joyful celebration of and delight in our sexuality," the Presbyterian statement continues:

> Interpersonal relationships of any kind whatsoever, marital or not, should enhance rather than limit the spiritual freedom

of the individuals involved. They should be vehicles of expressing that love which is commanded in the New Testament, the
compassionate and consistent concern for the well-being of the
other. They should provide for the upbuilding of the creative
potential of persons who are called to the task of stewardship
of God's world. They should occasion that joy in his situation,
which is one of man's chief means of glorifying his Creator.
They should open to persons that flow of grace which will enable them to bear their burdens without despair.

The perennial human values expressed so succinctly in these
paragraphs have been more or less echoed in other statements
from church groups and individual theologians. Among these
are statements by the British Council of Churches, by an English group of Friends (Quakers), by the Jesuit, Thomas Wass-
mer and theologian, Joseph Fletcher, by the former Anglican
archbishop of Canterbury, Archbishop Fisher, by Bishop John
A. T. Robinson, author of HONEST TO GOD, by Michael
Valente, former chairman of theology at Seton Hall University, and especially by Rustum and Della Roy in their book
and many articles on marital ethics and the future of marriage.
In all these cases the emphasis has been on a critical distinction between exploitative, depersonalizing relationships on
one hand and community promoting, mutual growth oriented
relations that respect the individual's integrity on the other
hand.

This said about ethics and values, let me shift my exploration for a moment into the political and economic spheres, and
suggest some possible repercussions there for our revolutionary reproductive technology and social acceptance of pluralism in male/female relations and parenthood.

Those under the age of twenty-five are the first generation
in human history to grow up in a contraceptive culture. This
fundamental fact has triggered a major psychological
revolution in America that Marshall McLuhan and George B.
Leonard have summed up as a shift from hot, intense,
genital/intercourse/orgasm oriented sexuality and images to a
more diffused, more sensual, "cool sex." I would like to take this
distinction one step further into the area of politics and economics.

Earlier I mentioned that our conception of marital fidelity

as sexual or genital exclusively arose from a moral and psychological framework that viewed the wife and unmarried daughter as the property of the husband or father. We are now shifting away from this hot sex approach to sexual ethic and marital fidelity as women become social persons in their own right. But we are also now faced with several other, I believe related, cultural inversions. As the younger generation, and society in general, move from hot sexual images to cool sex, as we transcend the traditional concept of wife as property "taken out of circulation" and accept the validity and even necessity of levels of intimacy outside the couple as support to this relation, are we not also witnessing a parallel and interrelated shift from hot to cool economics? Our "capitalistic" American culture grants prime emphasis to the acquisition of more and more "properties." I suspect that the impact of a diffused cool sexuality among today's youth is related in some way to their rejection of hot competitive, property oriented economics, their lack of concern in many cases for acquiring more and more material goods, a second car, a plush suburban home and all the needless accouterments of the good life.

I find it intriguing that many so-called primitive societies, particularly those of the American natives, north and south, have a very diffused sense of sexuality—they often have no word for adultery because the wife is not property of the husband and no word for illegitimate child because the infant is not considered property of a father or of its parents, it is automatically a member of the whole community. But these people match this cool sex with an equally cool economic system. In place of our hierarchical, funnel or pyramid structures in which the individual asserts his own uniqueness and identity by climbing over the corpses of his competitors, these "primitive societies" recognize the differences of individuals as complementary rather than competitive within the community. Property, beyond the bare personal essentials, is often communal and the emphasis is on communal cooperation rather than acquisitive competition.

A key question then in terms of political structures and economics is this: as we begin to accept a cool sexuality and pluralism in male/female relations, are we not also laying the foundation for a new conception of our political and economical structures, based on pluralistic, collegial and process-oriented structures rather than monolithic, hierarchical and fixed structures? Will the emphasis in all areas of life tomorrow, in the global tribe, be more on persons than on property, more on cooperation and less on competition?

I have only touched on some of the many questions posed by our reproductive technology and its anticipated social repercussions, but I hope I have highlighted some of the crucial and more important questions.

In the long term, I am convinced that all the turmoil of our present apocalyptic era, all its tensions—which are far more intense for men than for women—all its chaos, groping and confusion, will in the end result in a more human society, a more personal society, a more creative society and one certainly more adaptable to the exigencies of our rapidly changing environment.

Some Readings

Cuber, John F., and Harroff, Peggy B. *The Significant Americans: A Study of Sexual Behavior Among the Affluent.* New York: Appleton-Century-Crofts, 1965.

Francoeur, Robert T. *Evolving World, Converging Man.* New York: Holt, Rinehart and Winston, 1970.

———.*Utopian Motherhood: New Trends in Human Reproduction.* New York: Doubleday, 1970; Cranbury, N.J.: A. S. Barnes, 1972.

———. *Eve's New Rib: 20 Faces of Sex, Marriage and Family.* New York: Harcourt, Brace, Jovanovich, 1972.

McLuhan, Marshall, and Leonard, George B. "The Future of Sex." *Look Magazine,* July 25, 1967.

Neubeck, Gerhard, Ed. *Extramarital Relations.* Englewood Cliffs, N.J.: Prentice-Hall, Spectrum Books, 1969.

O'Neill, Nena and George. *Open Marriage: A New Life Style for Couples.* New York: M. Evans–J. P. Lippincott, 1972.

Otto, Herbert A., Ed. *The Family in Search of a Future: Alternate Models for Moderns.* New York: Appleton-Century-Crofts, 1970.

The United Presbyterian Church in the U.S.A., "Sexuality and the

Human Community." A task-force document issued by the 182nd General Assembly, Philadelphia, 1970.

Richardson, Herbert W. *Nun, Witch, Playmate: The Americanization of Sex.* New York: Harper and Row, 1971.

Rimmer, Robert H. *The Harrad Experiment.* New York: Bantam Books, 1967.

————. *Proposition 31.* New York: New American Library, Signet, 1969.

————. *The Rebellion of Yale Marratt.* New York: Avon Books, 1967.

————. *Thursday, My Love.* New York: New American Library, W. W. Norton, 1972.

Roy, Rustum and Della. *Honest Sex: A Revolutionary New Sex Ethics for the Now Generation of Christians.* New York: New American Library, Signet, 1958.

————. "Is Monogamy Outdated?" *The Humanist,* March-April, 1970.

Toffler, Alvin. *Future Shock.* New York: Random House, 1970.

RELIGIOUS HOPE AND TECHNOLOGICAL PLANNING

kenneth vaux

———————————— KENNETH VAUX ————————————

How does one relate the religious faith and hope of the human heart to man's technological venture? Does that envisioned new world and society have any connection with what he seeks to do with his technology? Can the prophetic discontents with the dehumanism of our culture, and the poignant hopes for a better world which grow out of our anger, somehow be implemented in concrete technological acts? These are the questions this essay seeks to explore. Jørgen Randers rightly calls on the churches and synagogues to bear a special burden for generating the commitments and sustaining the vision necessary to save and heal our world. This exploration seeks to discover the hopes, rooted in religious faith, which can strengthen that endeavor.

RELIGIOUS HOPE AND TECHNOLOGICAL PLANNING

When a human being is at his best he hopes and cares. He has a picture of what could be. He sees the disparity between his hope and what, in fact, is. Then he sets out to do something about it. Man cares with his will and with his action.

The things man makes enable him to care, with effect. Technology is the extension of man's active personality. It is swept into the sphere of value because through the technical capacities of power, and technique, man is achieving the capacity to care, effectively. He can see pain and do something about it.

The impulses to hope and to care are both born in a spiritual dimension of life. I have power to affirm another only because I am affirmed. That is a grace. Grace is spiritual energy released within man from beyond man. I administer immediate care because of ultimate concern. Before I can care, though, I must have a lively hope that things matter—that there is meaning. I care because I believe it makes a difference. Man must find the will to believe and hope. So religion and technology—the capacity to care and to do something about it—are intertwined concerns. Religious hope is that power by which man accepts and affirms the possible. Kierkegaard called it "a passion for the possible." Technology is the power by which man claims and actualizes hope.

The thesis I would explore is that religious hope and technological planning are integral concerns. I develop the argument as follows: I would speak first of the interpenetration of religious hope and technological planning, noting the historical roots and the contemporary interplay. I then want to suggest how several alienations of modern man can be understood within a hope symbol of biblical eschatology. Understood through religious hope, these disorders prompt us to a technological task. In other words, hope enables us to know something is wanting in the present and therefore possible in the future. Hope in the promised future of God makes us discontented with the present for the sake of that new possibility.

Let me illustrate this thesis with an example from the concern of each of the distinguished colleagues on this symposium. I will take the theme of *dominion* from Randers' work on global management; the theme of *competence* from Illich in his work on deschooling and retooling; from Francoeur and his work on sexuality, I choose the theme of *intimacy;* the theme of *health* I draw from Murray. These four human powers, presently distorted and alienated, are central themes in the religious hope for a new and possible world. Hope, as Jürgen Moltmann (author of THEOLOGY OF HOPE) has shown, entails both tension and a task, a contradiction and a commitment. The symbols I choose reflect this ambiguity.

HISTORICAL COINCIDENCE

First, a comment on the historical coincidence of religious hope and technology. The studies of this coincidence, particularly those of Van Leeuwen, Weizsäcker and Whitehead,[1] are well known. In religious hope man has always longed for a new world or a better world. Down through history, these hopes have fostered attitudes of both world negation and world affirmation, both withdrawal and creative planning. Some have sought the better life beyond this world; others seek utopia here and now. We are all painfully familiar with the many "otherworldly projections" that have so often borne out George Bernard Shaw's warning, "Beware of the man whose God is in the sky." Man has often been so obsessed with the heavenly city that he has shirked responsibility for the city of man. There can be eschatological hope without planning, for man generally waits for the kingdom, but there can be no planning without hope. Man cannot sustain any energy to plan a better world without vision.

Where the world view is cyclic, where the myth of eternal return controls consciousness, there can be no history. The only technology that emerges is decorative, as in the oriental gardens. It has been argued that a cyclic world view or a view of the earth as eternal makes for a better ecological theology. Such a view, it is argued, engenders a rhythmic harmony of man with nature rather than the dominating transcendence over nature that characterizes Western thought.

Although this dichotomy grossly distorts the biblical meaning of man's dominion in the cosmos,[2] it rightly points up that it is the Jewish faith, then Christian hope that gives the world a linear view of history and a disenchanted view of nature, the two prerequisites for planning and technology. Fred Polak, in his sociological study, *Image of the Future*,[3] has shown the way that Judaism combined in its hope the vision of supernatural Zion with man's responsibility for creating it here on the earth. In the covenant where God and man contract to build his kingdom on the earth, religious hope, based on God's promise, prompts the act of technical care, of planning.

Something happened in the eighteenth and nineteenth

centuries that cast a dark shadow on religious hope. It went far deeper than Freud and Marx. Our present crisis in hope and planning was born in the eschatological denial that characterized the enlightenment. The beyond is an illusion. The projected future is an instrument of economic exploitation. The nineteenth century saw man becoming autonomous and self-sufficient and God withdrawing from the shores of human life. Man in his possibility and tragedy is the ultimate reality. *Nietzsche* poses the modern point of despair, the death of hope:

> Whither does the earth now move? Whither do we move? Away from all suns? Backwards, sideways, forwards, in all directions? Is there still an above or below? Do we not stray, as through infinite nothingness? Does not empty space breathe upon us? [4]

The legacy lingers today. Hope comes hard, and where there is no vision the people perish. The contemporary question is framed by Elise Boulding: "Can humanistic Utopia (which includes hopeful planning) survive the death of eschatology?" [5] Can man continue to plan and build after he has lost hope?

Another historical current has practical importance today. Weizsäcker, in DIE EINHEIT DER NATUR (THE HISTORY OF NATURE, Munich, 1971), argues that roots of modern science grow from Greek philosophy as much as from Hebrew-Christian cosmology. This part of our tradition affirms the rationality of the cosmos. Although this world view often saw reality in static ways and became non-progressive, it has profoundly affected the emergence of science and technology. Only the world that can be understood can be planned. Only where cause and effect and predictability can be trusted, can there be planning. Albert Einstein expressed this faith when he said; "The Lord God may be subtle, but he isn't just plain mean." Hope or confidence in cosmic predictability and progressive knowledge are what sustain technological planning. Einstein called it faith. Chesterton called it the assurance we have that the Lord says to the sun every morning "get up now" and to the moon every night "come on—get up." Both the idea of historical purposiveness and of cosmic predictability—roots that alone can sustain the growth of technological care and planning—are grounded in religious hope. Polak has said ". . . eschatology is the oratorium of religious fulfillment, and Utopia is the laboratorium of social process." [6] The religious community today has the task of affirming the cosmos as rational and providential, the confidences that alone can activate hope.

On the basis of this thesis let us take four examples of a current human alienation or disorder, examine each in the light of a hope symbol, and see what technical task emerges.

DOMINION

Man today is deeply uncertain as to what his dominion in the cosmos means. Down through the ages he has felt constrained and compelled to "subdue the earth" to protect and to enrich his life. In his hope for less pain and more comfort, he has contorted the vitalities of nature to his own purposes. He has exerted control over animal and plant; over earth and atmosphere; over matter and energy. Indeed, he has sought to organize all nature through the nexus of his mind and will.

Now the process is in vicious recoil against him. Nature seems to howl. The white duck washes ashore covered with black oil, the pines east of the Rockies start to rust and die. The cities consume and devour human life. The microbiotic and insect worlds gather strength as they mutate against man's defenses. One wonders indeed whether the cockroach will have the last word. Human wealth and misery seem to multiply together. Man exhausts natural and energy resources far in excess of earth's recuperative powers. His dominion sours into domination.

Yet both his memory and his hope speak of a *garden*. Here creatures dwell in harmony. Here man tills the earth, instrumentally allowing nature her purpose which is, in part, the filling of his needs. Here earth brings forth her bread, the vine her grape. Here wolf dwells at peace with the lamb as all creatures in harmonious synergy enhance one another and call one another into being. Memory and hope in this religious sense not only speak of what the world could be like, but what it should be like: hope carries responsibility. Moltmann says:

Those who hope (in Christ) can no longer put up with reality as it is, but begin to suffer under it to contradict it. Peace with God means conflict with the world, for the good of the promised future stabs inexorably into the flesh of every unfulfilled present.[7]

How do we translate the symbol of a garden or of a peaceable kingdom into technical responsibility? It would be just as wrong to consider it a blueprint for technological planning as it would to see it as wholly otherworldly. Jørgen Randers proposes to us in his essay the equilibrium state as the harbinger of a golden age for mankind. This goal will be accomplished by a curtailing of physical and populational growth until an equilibrium of resource and utilization, of need and satisfaction, is achieved. Only when we achieve this harmony of man and ecosystem will a cataclysm be averted and peace and health be possible. The technical task we are called to is quite simple: allow the world her natural possibility; do not stir her up in a Toffler-like momentum so that she collapses from exhaustion and fails to carry her life. Religious hope dreams of that equilibrium state and does something about it. As Randers has said, probably only the church can produce both the long-range time-horizon and the moral courage to act. I would want to define the church here in New Testament fashion as the community of those who wait, hope and serve. The church knows that God is redemptively fashioning his creation. His people cooperate in anger and in action.

COMPETENCE

Mr. Illich uses the marvelous image of *conviviality*. May I slightly construe his point and talk of competence? A fundamental alienation of man today occurs in his failure to be able to do for himself and others what is good and necessary. Man today has become self-alienated in that he has lost the competence to constrain the environment creatively to his needs. He has been forced into alienation by systems that feed on consumption. Illich calls conviviality "individual freedom realized in mutual personal interdependence." If any disorder is acute in modern mass society, it is the inability to master circumstance, to hold oneself together, to keep integrity and inner-directedness against a culture based on control, to effectively serve and honor one's fellow man. We see ourselves swept along by incontrollable forces. One must struggle to stay above water in the stream of economic momentum. If nerve fails, we wash under or drift ashore to become the driftwood on the waves of materialistic forces.

Education is one of our key motifs in this conference. Today many people see education as a decompensating process where our children are taught to neglect or repress their inbred creativity and potential competence. Children are taught that they cannot teach themselves. Parents are told that their children must learn from the hands of experts. We might add that teachers are continually reminded in professional circles of their incompetence. In THE PETER PRINCIPLE the author argues that one rises to the level of incompetence, then stalls. In theology and the ministry, for example, the priests and pastors flounder at sea in a crisis of personal and vocational identity. One cannot teach the Bible—only biblical scholars can do that. One cannot do theology—that's for theologians. Counseling? better leave it to the psychologist. Healing? that's for psychiatrists and doctors. Social advocacy? that's for social and political scientists, and the folks don't like it anyway. A professional trauma of incompetence. This trauma may be good in that it teaches the priest what he shouldn't try to be; but it concerns me when it immobilizes him as an instrument of the Spirit to help and heal people.

There is a strong biblical metaphor called *work*. It is one of religion's most interesting eschatological symbols. Man remembers that he worked in paradise, tilling the garden. It was not toil, but joy. The Bible symbolizes the present alienation of man from his labor in man's sweat for bread and woman's anguish in childbirth.

Religious memory and hope also knows of a *homeland*. Here man's bondage is released, his work finished, his journey over. Here the land willingly yields up her goodness. The oppressed know this hope best. They also know the radical political meaning of that hope. The spiritual song of the American black, the poetry of Fanon, Mondlane, Torres, Guevara cry it. Ernst Bloch from the crucible of European Marxism speaks of it. The homeland is the historical overcoming of what Tillich calls the proletarian situation, where some men are controlled by others by the sale of their bodies and labor. It is release from having one's destiny determined by the turn of the market. It is leisure in Calvin's beautiful sense of that word. It is release to competence.

Karl Marx, standing in the biblical prophetic tradition, talked of *entfremdete arbeit,* alienated work. In this productive process man is separated from the tangible result of his work, his neighbor and fundamentally his own being. For Marx, alienation meant literally being torn from one's ground, cut off, in the oriental sense, from being and meaning. Thus estranged, one becomes a passive tool; what has been called the "other-directed" person, the nobody with no center, no competence. This is the man whose needs are created by advertising, by vested interests. He lives by fulfilling expectations, rather than by creating a life and a personal cosmos.

Mr. Illich has developed the powerful cultural meaning of this alienation and the hope and task necessary to overcome it. Religious hope envisions a new being, a new society, a new world where men are set free from work as toil and alienation, to work as creativity and competence. Religious hope exists in the lively interaction with that technical task. I have argued elsewhere that cybernation technology can exonerate man's mind and will from production in the same way that automation exonerates his body.[8] It is also evident that communications technology has great potential for self education and competence building. The technical task is one of redirecting our technology for those goals. The most powerful message entrusted to the church is that grace releases man from strife and self-justification and renders him competent to the greatest challenge and possibility he can imagine.

INTIMACY

Dr. Francoeur has challenged our ideas and values with his discussion of technology and sexuality. Alienation from one's sexual being is acute today. Freud and his followers have suggested that a broad cultural repression has accompanied this personal disorder. We now play frantic games—encounter groups, sensitivity sessions, excitements of dance and play and other expressions—trying to rediscover that lost self, that primitive being who can feel and love. We struggle to find the purpose of sexuality no longer able to bear procreation as its single meaning. We struggle to understand the role of male and female. Today male and female are matters of degree. The poles differentiate in a broad spectrum yielding all kinds of "strange aberrations" from celibacy to homosexuality to transsexuality, exceptions that we have trouble incorporating into our system. In all the crises in our society related to sexuality, we find expression of alienation in the sphere of intimacy. How can we know and love and share at the deepest interpersonal level without destroying ourselves and without destroying the other?

Religious hope knows of *koinonia*. This fellowship is self-giving and self-fulfilling because it is rooted in God. He creates *koinonia* through his self-giving. Knowledge and intimacy join in a unitive act of care in that life that can be. The Bible knows no deeper way to speak of God's care for man than *yahda* (intercourse) and *xaris* (grace) which in the Hebrew means literally the cry of a mother camel for her offspring lost in the desert. Jesus calls us friends. He fashions a new humanity where there is no male or female, where equity and reciprocity govern human affairs. In this hope we overcome alienation as through acceptance we call one another into being.

The technical task here is that of making intimacy possible. The earth has long forced man into aggressive territoriality and war as he has had to farm and build and conquer to control environment. Perhaps through technology a new *man* can be born, one whose strength is gentle, whose purpose is not to subdue and seduce but to care. Perhaps *woman* can be released from her toil. Her domesticity, in the worst sense of that word, involving passivity, and receptivity and resentment, can be lifted. Perhaps the anguish of war vigil, of child bearing, of drudgery to sustain life can be transformed so that she lives to share the unfolding life of the young and the old in the family and express her full range of gifts. Technology, of course, cannot do this. But religious hope and technological planning can. New levels of intimacy can be fashioned in our world as community becomes the presence of shared hope.

HEALTH

The ultimate negation of man's hope is disease and death. The current excitement over medical technology and, most recently, genetic technology is merely the intensification of this hope/despair dialectic.

Robert Murray has illustrated the way in which a thirst for life with spontaneity and hope is impinged upon by modern genetic knowledge. Is hope shattered by too much knowledge? Is rigid prognosis always to be preferred over blind acceptance of the unknown? If parents have the right to bring deformed children into the world, what are the rights of those children? All of these issues of genetic imperfection and neonatal malformation raise the larger normative questions of man's search for health, wholeness, salvation.

In genetic knowledge science pursues not only creation and correction of human substance but the processes of aging. Do 100,000 brain neurons have to die every day after the age of 35? Man's alienation from wholeness and health has prompted a frantic search for the fountain of youth, salvation and immortality. Man cannot accept the apparent fact that he is born to suffer and die. His hope tells him that he should not die. His hope convinces him that much disease and premature death are unnecessary—the fault of his own ignorance and malice.

Yet man knows that he must die. Indeed he knows his death to be part of a greater wisdom. René Dubos has convincingly shown how health is a mirage. Man's longing for a golden age, a paradise, a Tahiti, a Parousia is good and natural; but this hope could not be actualized. If it were realized, human life would cease, developmental evolution would be thwarted. Pain and struggle might be averted, but it would mean species death.

But in memory and hope man knows of a peace. Not extinction or obliteration, but peace. Just as in the dreaming innocence of his memory he knows that he did not die, he hopes for the coming day of no pain—no tears—no death. What an uncanny anticipation for this "accidental collection of atoms destined to extinction in the vast death of the solar system." [9] The symbol that sustains this hope is *resurrection*. It is the most persistent eschatological symbol in human history. It is a symbol active and pervasive in "times of troubles" like ours when mystery religions, cults and apocalypticisms prevail. The symbol loses power somewhat in good times and healthy seasons. Yet it persists. For the Jew it is witnessed in the persistent Phoenix-like regeneration of a people from the ashes. It is sustained by the faithfulness of God who leads his people out. Among Christians it is sustained by resurrection faith in a Man, who despite D. H. Lawrence's warning, is not "a past number." In Jesus Christ, Man humiliates death. Through his divine operation, lively hope is born even in the midst of tragic history.

The technical task in response to this hope may be hubris and even blasphemy. It means nothing less than an all-out effort to defeat those forces that inflict disease, debilitation and death. We set out on this road the minute the preacher said the plague was the will of God and we laughed in his face. The theodicy problem no longer immobilizes us. Why do children die of cancer if God is good? The pain of that question spurs us to action. We act defiantly in the face of ultimate futility. We rage against the dying of the light.

Our task today is to translate this great hope and resultant technical energy into a universal accomplishment. We cannot rest while one still suffers or dies who would not suffer or die if we cared.

On the gates of Dante's Inferno is a placard that reads: "All hope abandon, ye who enter here." As long as man has hope, he will not enter that hell. If his hope is joined with *care*ful technical action, he will endure and prevail. If hope or care fail, he surely will plunge into utter darkness.

Footnotes

1. Arend Van Leeuwen, *Christianity in World History* (New York: Scribners), 1964; Carl von Weizäcker, *The History of Nature* (Chicago: University of Chicago Press), 1949; Alfred North Whitehead, *Science and the Modern World* (New York: Macmillan), 1925.

2. Kenneth Vaux, *Subduing the Cosmos* (Richmond, Va.: John Knox Press), 1970.

3. Fred L. Polak, *The Image of the Future*. Translated by Elise Boulding (New York: Braziller), 1971.

4. Friedrich Nietzsche, *The Gay Science* in Walter Kaufmann *The Portable Nietzsche* (New York: The Viking Press), 1954, p. 95.

5. Elise Boulding, "Religious Awareness and Images of the Future" presented at the annual meeting of the Society for the Scientific Study of Religion, 1970. (Supplied by the author.)

6. Fred L. Polak, *op. cit.*, p. 61.

7. Jürgen Moltmann, *Theology of Hope* (New York: Harper and Row), 1964, p. 25.

8. Kenneth Vaux, *op. cit.*

9. Bertrand Russell, *A Free Man's Worship: Mysticism and Logic* (London: George Allen), 1939, p. 93.

COMMENTARY

the faculty of the institute of religion and human development

THE REFLECTION OF A
PHILOSOPHER-POLITICAL SCIENTIST
BENEDICT ASHLEY, O.P., Ph.D.

In our rapidly changing society all of us sometimes need wise counsel in trying to make decisions in situations in which traditional norms do not provide clear answers. Among the available counselors, the minister, priest or rabbi are the ones to whom many of us turn, because we know that the psychiatrist, the doctor, the lawyer, the social-worker may be of great assistance, but they are not of much help at the point where the question "right" and "wrong," the strictly ethical question is raised.

If the minister of religion is to meet expectations of good ethical counsel, he must realize that individual decisions always have a social context. What we decide to do must either seek social support, or must be a conscientious resistance to accepted social patterns. Jørgen Randers, in his paper, clearly indicates one of the basic questions of social policy that we now must face. If he is right, then, the "American way of life," that is, that of two-thirds of our population and to which most of the other third is making a claim, must be rejected and a new scale of values put in its place.

Whenever we counsel an American we are probably dealing with someone whose goal is "success in life" measured by the ideal of an ever-growing economy, an ever higher standard of living. This goal is a basic determinant of every moral decision he makes. Randers is saying that if we continue to make this type of decision, then in one or two generations our civilization will collapse. If we believe that we have an obligation to future generations, then in the United States and other developed countries we must begin systematically to limit the growth of the economy, just as we have already in fact begun to limit the growth of our population. This latter limitation must also be spread to the undeveloped countries. This means, as I see it, a very marked "transvaluation of values" that affects almost every counseling situation with which the minister of religion deals. If he accepts Randers' argument, he will make it an aim in each situation to ask his clients: "Could you at this point plan your life so as to live more modestly, with lower consumption of goods, and therefore, with a search for satisfaction of a different kind?" We are back to the Gospel words, "Seek you first the kingdom of God, and the other things will be added."

Randers argues that the basic ethical decision is whether we should live for the short-run or the long-run. Even in the days when Christians believed that there was only going to be a short-run before the Second Advent, St. Paul indicated this did not dispense them from the duty to keep the world going. Furthermore, for the Christian, future generations are part of the one human family that must live for each other forever. There can be no hesitation, therefore, as to the Christian duty to live by the rule proposed by Randers, "that no man or institution in our society may take any action that decreases the economic and social options of those who will live on the planet over the next 100 years."

I feel however that ethics does raise a difficulty about the short-run and long-run that Randers does not take into account. In making a decision ethically we must consider the consequences of an action. What do we do when some consequences are certain or highly probable, others less probable? Obviously, a prudent decision must rest more on certain consequences than on probable ones, although it cannot ignore the latter. This means that in the here-and-now decisions must rest more on short-term consequences that are more predictable, and less on long-term consequences that are, in general,

less predictable. It would be foolish, therefore, to adopt measures (e.g. compulsory sterilization or infanticide of defec-
tives) that *certainly* violate individual freedom and the dignity of the person in the short-run, in order to prevent
probable long-run overpopulation. I feel we must insist on this
principle lest in becoming sensitive to our obligation to the future at which we guess, we become insensitive to the rights of
people in the present whose needs we certainly know.

We need to ask, therefore, if to protect the future we are
permitted to limit or even reduce the "quality of life" for
Americans now alive. As soon as we raise that question the
ambiguity of that term "quality of life" becomes evident and it
is with this that Illich deals in his contrast between "conviviality" and "productivity," a contrast similar to the "Consciousness III" and "Consciousness II" of Charles A. Reich. Again it
is obvious that the Christian gospel gives priority to "conviviality" over "productivity," to a life based not on production
and consumption of material goods, but on material simplicity,
personal freedom, the sharing of wealth and work, and the
pursuit of contemplative truth. However, we are left wonder-
ing if Illich is right in believing that it is possible to develop a
technology that by-passes the hierarchical, centralized pattern
of industrialism in favor of wide-spread, non-professional access to sources of technical information and simple tools. Will
this work?

Since we really do not know and Illich's arguments are
hardly more than suggestions, it seems to me that public policy (governmental or extra-governmental) should attempt serious and extensive *experimentation* as part of Randers'
general movement to limit economic growth. The best places
for such experimentation would seem to be undeveloped
countries: but it should also begin in developed countries.

Such changes in our life style are obviously bound up with
the problem of the nuclear family and of modern sexuality to
which Robert Francoeur addresses himself by proposing some
twenty options in place of the single approved model of heterosexual monogamy. In the controversy over Pope Paul VI's
Humanae Vitae, the Catholic defenders of contraception generally argued that the Pope was mistaken in thinking that
contraception necessarily separates procreation from sexuality,

since contraception can be used to promote family welfare. Francoeur, a Catholic, sweeps this aside and frankly accepts the separation not only as a fact, but apparently as morally legitimate. This puts him on the side of Paul VI who warned that contraception would open the way to many of the options proposed by Francoeur that Christian moralists of the past and present generally reject.

In my opinion Francoeur's paper suffers from a basic ambiguity. He speaks of "option" as if this means not only "technologically feasible" but also "morally permissible" or "humanly valuable." I do not see how homosexual marriage has been made an option in either sense by the advances in reproductive technology. Certainly modern psychology has persuaded most moralists that society ought to be much more compassionate about the homosexual's condition, but it is by no means certain that this condition should be treated as an "option" open to moral choice in a way that heterosexual monogamous marriage is an "option." I realize that this is a question open to argument, but the argument will have to move on a very different level of consideration than the simple question of technological feasibility discussed by Francoeur. His "options" are all highly debatable (otherwise why the debate about celibacy?) and the issues involved are more psychological and interpersonal than they are biological or technological.

Why ethical questions cannot be merely technical becomes very clear in Robert Murray's paper, which is so sensitive to the human dimension, as well as to the dilemmas produced by new but inadequate scientific information. To me, Murray's general position seems sound because he begins with the fundamental assumption that it is in the best interests of society to maximize the power of people to make informed decisions about their choice of partners and their family planning. Randers might object that this ignores "long-term" responsibilities, but I think it does not, since a good society is one that maximizes this personal freedom now and in the future. Certainly it is not demonstrated that people, given adequate counseling, will not freely plan reproduction in a way that will prevent major social disaster.

Murray asks if it is ethical for persons willingly to remain ignorant of possible genetic consequences. In general, willful ignorance in important matters is always irresponsible, yet in the *present* state of genetic knowledge and technological control, it is not clear that persons have a duty to inquire, when this inquiry may not really be of much practical help. I would agree, therefore, with Murray that laws obliging genetic examination are at present of dubious value.

I believe also that we should not foster magical-thinking about our control over the future. The element of risk in bringing children into the world cannot be wholly eliminated, since they are human persons subject to fate and fortune and free autonomous choice. The parent who will accept only the kind of child he wants can never be a good parent. It would seem, therefore, that it is only those cases where the risk of a seriously deformed child is very high, that would fall properly under human control. In such cases the counselor has the obligation to help the parents make a decision on the basis of the best information available. He also has the obligation as a human being and a professional concerned with persons to impart this information and to give support of a kind that will enable the clients to make a decision that is as rational, free and authentic as possible, so that they can live with their decision. This requires on the counselor's part great respect for the client's capacity to make decisions according to his own standards and values, even if these differ from the counselor's values.

I would add that since I believe direct abortion to be destructive of the fundamental obligation of society to protect the individual, including the fetus, which is at least an individual living entity in the process of personalization, I believe that a counselor should also do what he can to protect the unborn child from the parent's possible desire to destroy it, as he would attempt to protect that child once born.

With my colleague, Kenneth Vaux, I would argue that in the face of the moral anguish presented by a society where growing technological control gives man more and more power, yet seems to leave him helpless before the unwillingness of the human community to agree on positive solutions to questions of social policy, that hope must be the basic attitude with which we confront every decision.

THE REFLECTION OF A MEDICAL STUDENT
MICHAEL HEMPHILL

The papers presented here have dealt with the preservation of human values in the face of rapid technological change. They reflect our recognition that we are in a new era of ethical thinking. Whereas reflection on human values has always been man's attempt to understand himself and where he fits into the nature of things, his reflection today will directly influence the quality of life for himself and his progeny. As Dr. Francoeur stated, the present technological revolution is most characterized by its rapidity. Decisions must be made as to its course with appropriate attentiveness, or we will have little say as to how our lives will be altered by its efficiency. Reflective thinking has always pondered the questions of "What is good?" or "What is truth?" or "What is the nature of existence?" In these times we must make use of our reflective skills in determining "What is preferable?"

Each of our authors has chosen values he feels should be most cherished, and each has shown not only how these values may be maintained in a technological era, but how they may be enriched. Ivan Illich has emphasized the imperatives of conviviality and autonomy. He insists that in dealing with his fellow man and with his environment, man is most himself when he keeps the extensions of his self to a minimum. The more one removes himself from the challenges of subsistence —by confining himself to one segment and allowing other persons or devices to act for him elsewhere—the more he cuts away at his own humanity. Jørgen Randers has brought out that man dehumanizes life for future generations when he acts for his own immediate gratification without taking responsibility for long-term consequences. Dr. Francoeur has lent an air of optimism and excitement in the realm of interpersonal relations when he shows how bio-technology can wean man away from genitality and exclusivity as the essential components of intimacy, making way for greater freedom of exploration among adults who love each other. Dr. Murray has given us a constellation of five values to be uppermost when one has the power through bio-technology to give information that may alter the course of another person's choice of mate or choice to give birth. Dr. Vaux then takes the primacy of human caring and shows that in a variety of technological areas, technological planning can lead man to insure the promises of his religious hope.

One of the areas most frequently referred to in considering the consequences of technological advancement is that of health care. Illich makes a case for the despecialization of medical delivery and for the establishment of criteria for the maximum as well as minimum quantity of medical services a civilization should expect. He makes his case in the context of "radical politics" and in doing so highlights a critical point: in a democracy, the basic decisions regarding the usage of technology will be decided politically—by the wishes of the general public. Although the precise guidelines for what is an essential and what is a dehumanizing level of medical intervention will be decided administratively by sophisticated consultants, the decision of *whether* to guarantee these guidelines will be based on the moral feelings of the general populace.

Already we have found considerable dissension in the public mind in the area of national health insurance. Although this is a more proximal goal than that of Illich's radical politics and falls within the realm of the "reactionary," it is a course that nevertheless must be run. Shall our society, with its increasing capacity to insure protection from life-threatening disease, take measures to see that all its people are guaranteed this protection? If so, there is a basic ethical barrier that must be hurdled in the public mind for its insurance. The advantaged and affluent of the society must be willing to defer their historical role of *noblesse oblige* and recognize that those who have not been regular recipients of technological fruits have a right to demand them.

This is an issue not peculiar to a technological era, but for the first time it is an ever-present one that must not be accompanied by revolution at each new turn. In the past the outcry of the have-nots has not been tolerated because the means for meeting their demands has been limited or would considerably detract from the accustomed standard of living of the haves. For example, with a limited number of physicians and laboratory tools, ready access to health care could not really be demanded simply because the demand far exceeded the supply. As we know, in a free enterprise system the supply goes to those capable of offering remuneration. In this situation, the disposition of those incapable of affording the precious services was left to the charity of the affluent. This was a comfortable position reinforced by our traditional, biblical ethic, as we shall see. In our present age, however, a so-called crisis has arisen, not because the situation is any worse for the poor, but because the means are now available for rapidly increasing levels of provision. And when the means become available, a more informed group of have-not peoples feel no need to wait upon the charity of the advantaged.

The biblical admonition is to heal the sick, to clothe the naked, to feed the poor. It speaks to those capable of doing the providing and places the responsibility on them. This has been a satisfactory approach to the affluent throughout history. Whereas responsibility is left to them, the initiative is left to them, also. In a technological society, however, we shall find that issues which have traditionally been deeds of charity and goodwill will become expected and enforceable rights. The fact that they will be demanded by the irrepressible outcry of the unprivileged is certain. Yet the mood of the present American population—as reflected by the rightward shift of political opinion—is toward a suppression of demands upon society's benefits.

We will move toward a decreased tendency to rely upon the affluent to apportion out technological fruits. In the pattern of our five authors, we must recognize basic human values and accord them to everyone. What these values are will depend on our answer to the question, "Who is man?" a question that will require all the reflective energies we can muster. Yet a reasonable consensus must be reached if we are to promote the dispersion of technological advancement without painful discord.

The question of "Who is man?" and the concomitant determinations of those qualities that make up human existence arise at yet another level of medical technology. It was reasoned above that the dispensing of medical care will become a matter of commitment to basic human values, to be expected by everyone and not left to the arbitrary discretion of the affluent. On another scale we are being called upon to determine the criteria of human life in providing medical care to individuals in complex medical situations.

Illich and others have objected that a disproportionate amount of medical research, funds and effort have been devoted to the simple prolongation of life. Illich states, "The majority of the cost of medical research and services rendered in United States hospitals go for what can be done or is done to patients during the last two years of their lives." He also says, "A society that defines medicine as the act of life extension deserves to be governed by economists who define themselves as the architects of sustained and unlimited growth." Illich leaves us with the feeling that it is he who is taking a statistical, economic viewpoint. For here we are discussing much more than the question of euthanasia, where a very personal decision, based on the feelings of the patient, loved ones, and the physician are involved. Illich's case is for unequivocal withdrawal of treatment to those who either have not long to live or who will be living at a lesser capacity than their accustomed one. One must assume that the qualities of life valued in that case are, in fact, productivity and function to society. A more humane hierarchy of values would instead state that to be loved and to maintain the capacity to perceive the world around him are more cherishable than the capacity to provide service to society, and are at best equal to the ability to act out one's desires with the benefit of normal function. A counter-comment to Illich's statement would say, "A society that defines medicine as the act of treating the productive deserves to be governed by economists who define themselves as the architects of sustained and unlimited growth."

Illich is implying that only those diseases that are certain to have a good prognosis should be treated. Such conditions are certainly within the range of any moderately trained person—minor infections and minor trauma, for example, and might be amenable to "tool kit" medicine. In a society where these kinds of problems are not being met, an insistence on their primacy is plausible. Where society is responding to these, and has, in addition, the means to "prolong life" with treatment of diabetes, coronary artery disease, hypertension and many tumors, however, it seems inhuman to deny them simply because they are complex diseases. The expense and technology required to treat them speaks more for the complexity of the disease process than the vested interest of the medical specialist. To turn away from their ominous presence in order to preserve our consumption of services and materials reverses our hierarchy of values: it places man as the servant of his economy. Illich parallels the preoccupation of death-avoidance with gross national product. On the contrary, the preoccupation with economics at the expense of human life is the more materialistic value orientation.

The question, then, of "Who is man?" leads us to affirm values of love, caring and the ability to experience; these are essential to human life. When one has not the ability to maintain these, we may then think in terms of euthanasia or refusal to treat that person. To hold back medical therapy in cases of treatable disease simply because they require sophisticated technology is to be reactionary and is a refusal to subordinate the tools of technology to the worthwhileness of life.

A brief response to a sentence in Illich's paper is in order. He states, "The doctor is trained to provide increasing pains at increasing cost, just as the economist stimulates increasing demand to produce increasing sales." It is obvious that there is no advantage to the physician nor to the health industry to provoke pain where the procedure or medication does not surpass the pain produced transiently with relief from disease. The possibility that the treatment may be worse than the disease is at the forefront of every physician's decision to order diagnostic tests or to prescribe therapy. To say that no physician has ever been guilty of poor judgment in this area is absurd; it is a matter of human judgment. To say that he is specifically trained to ignore it is equally absurd.

THE REFLECTION OF A PHYSICIAN
HARRY S. LIPSCOMB, M.D.

Technology, in either the broad or narrow sense, is not new. Neither does it demand more of human understanding than was required 2,000 years ago. What is true is that there is more technology, it is more liable to misuse and misunderstanding, and it has enriched the material life of our world, often without having broadened our spiritual growth. We have confused a product with a process, and have allowed what should have been a handmaiden of society to become the central focus of our needs, the primary reflection of our successes, and the final arbiter of human decisions. Major legislative action touching upon human values is derived from a cauldron of scientific knowledge whose ladle is controlled by technologists. Somehow in this process, there has evolved a peculiar philosophy that equates "hard," quantitative data with clear thinking, and "soft," empiric and intuitive judgment with opaque thought.

Earlier in this volume, Randers has emphasized that one need not be a scientist and understand the exact nature of mercury poisoning to speak out against pollution as an environmental evil. He is of course correct, but he apparently fails to recognize that legislative action in a modern society is controlled by a technocracy that has been maintained through the largesse of vast military and corporate interests whose survival depends upon a technologically-oriented, consumer economy.

For every new technological advance reflected by a marketable product, men of good will must impose valid criteria of need, and must balance need against utility. Utility must couple the concept of greatest good for greatest number, weighing the consequences of depletion of natural resources or contribution to non-recyclable refuse, and requiring that a product provide physical as well as material benefit to mankind.

If personal income and population go unchecked, Randers' model (an example of appropriate use of technology in information-theory and analog-computer modeling) predicts dire consequence for the world. Here the model ends, however, and reality begins. The reality is that no amount of technology can effectively alter these trends unless human decisions are made at a level that transcends scientific disciplines and the cult of technology. These are visceral, empiric, gut-level decisions that require courage in a technologically oriented society.

There is nothing more absurd than doing more efficiently what should never have been done at all, and technology is a case in point. Our machines and appliances save us time that we use in the consumption of more products, or the pursuit of goals which are in themselves destructive. Our medical equipment saves many lives that should never have been saved at all. We maintain a quantitative longevity of a life devoid of quality. Somewhere GNP and cost-benefit analysis have become deified, and the human spirit has suffered. Now, we wish to thrust this "better life" upon the underdeveloped nations of the world.

An examination of these nations, however, suggests that we have, through communications technology, persuaded them that our technological life style is, in all cases, desirable for them. In our addiction to the "abundant life," we seek to thrust our life style on our neighbors—provided they can pay the price.

It seems reasonable, therefore, that we might benefit from a reassessment of our present values to redefine simpler, more fundamental life styles. In the process of reclaiming those elements that bring fulfillment to man's soul, technology's role then becomes part of the structure of human survival.

The role of the interpreter and the conscience of our technology will best be served by those individuals who are continually aware of human needs. Their responsibilities will be heavy. It is in this role that the pastoral ministry can bring about the most humanistic approach to the application of technology. One might foresee, half in jest, the rise of yet another technocracy consisting of a humanitarian movement using organized media throughout the world. Working in concert such a group might well have an impact which reaches beyond the confines of the continental United States to become a world-wide movement. In reviewing the life of Gandhi, it became clear that an entire continent could be influenced by the ideas set forth and communicated broadly by a single man's conviction. This conviction must become pandemic. We have seen increasing national support to bring about the protection of our natural environment, and to foster a change in attitudes affecting disadvantaged groups. These changes in emphasis were generated not by industrial representatives, but by groups of concerned individuals. Some halting steps have finally been taken toward population control, again largely because of a social movement and not because of any progress in technology. For instance, new birth control measures have only changed the time base for dealing with a burgeoning world population.

Another proposal has its roots within organized religion. I can foresee a change in spiritual values transcending classic Judaeo-Christian ideas, coupling Western ethos to that of the East. Such a movement is not without precedent; the Renaissance engendered dramatic changes in man's world view.

Conferences of this sort, while they do not offer concrete solutions for the problems of "Technology and a Human Future," are useful and should be continued. In focusing upon these problems, the participants give witness to the world that concerned individuals exist, that they have thought deeply on these issues and are prepared to testify to their urgency.

THE REFLECTION OF A SCIENTIST
ALBERT S. MORACZEWSKI, O.P., Ph.D.

Like Adam and Eve, we stand at the threshold of a procreative revolution; or more accurately a procreative *and* a genetic revolution. It is procreative because it is becoming increasingly possible to separate *pro*creation from *re*creation. It is genetic because we have become increasingly aware of, and are able to do something about, genetic mishaps. But in both instances, because we can, *should* we? Now is the time for religious persons to ask that disturbing question.

There are some who say that technological changes—I say *changes* because all changes are not necessarily *advances*—are inevitable: what science and technology can do, it will inevitably do. If we admit this proposition, we are really admitting that we are not truly free, that we truly do not have control over the product of our brains and hands. Frankenstein's monster is loose again! This would be to deny in any practical sense the freedom not only of the individual man, but the freedom of society, and without freedom there can be no morality, no religion. But because I believe that man is fundamentally free in his moral choices, the following reflections are vitally important.

There is an urgent ethical and moral challenge that faces man: what is he going to do with the technology he has developed; will it control him or will he be its master? Not everything science can do, may it do. Merely having the power to do something does not give us the right to use that power. Merely because I have a pistol in my hand does not entitle me to kill somebody with it. I can choose to do so or not do so. Analogously, merely because a society has the technological power to do something, does not mean that it has the ethical right to use that power. (The use of nuclear energy to make a bomb is an example.) If man's greatness resides in anything, it seems to reside in the fact that he can freely choose to do or not to do; that he has the power to destroy but elects not to do so; that he has the means to change, but has also the freedom to decide whether that change would be truly beneficial.

As the Conference powerfully underlined, we are faced with critical ethical decisions: in planning for the good life, do we want to think only of our present generation or do we consider the yet unborn for the next 150 years (Randers)? Do we opt for or against a simpler and more human mode of life that gives each person the opportunity to function with creative and responsible freedom (Illich)? By controlling conception and birth, by deliberately modifying the genetic makeup of our offspring, shall we shape the characteristics of those who come after us (Francoeur and Murray)? In view of the godlike power that is becoming increasingly at our disposal, shall we humanize technology or de-technologize humanity (Vaux)? Each of these decisions is a massive problem.

Having said this, how do we make ethical decisions in such complex situations? For a person living in a Judaeo-Christian tradition, there are certain fundamental, moral "givens," that he can use as points of departure. It seems that the dignity and worth of the human person is one such moral value. Irrespective of the particular religious tradition in which a person stands there are many who would also propose that another moral criterion is the continuity of the human race. Anything that contributes towards that goal would be morally good and anything that would tend to work against that goal would be considered reprehensible. This standard is compatible with the Judaeo-Christian tradition since the realization of the eschatological kingdom presumes the continued presence of the human race. A possible conflict, however, may arise between the worth of the human person on the one hand and the continuation of the community on the other. Can one person be refused admission to an overcrowded life-raft in order that the others may survive? It does not seem possible to state a general principle which would resolve automatically every difficulty and conflict. It is of some help to recall that the dignity of the human person means that a person cannot be used as a mere means to a goal no matter how exalted and noble that goal may be.

The control of population required by Randers and the change of values implied by both Illich and Randers is approached biologically by Francoeur. Now that we have separated sex from procreation, he says, we can consider them independently of one another. Already in the experimental stage is the transplantation of human embryos.

Also related to population control but closer to current reality is genetic counseling discussed by Murray. At first sight we would probably all agree that removal of defective genes from the human gene pool is desirable. But it is conceivable that what we call a disease might in other circumstances be an advantage. For example, it seems that sickle cell anemia, which is found almost exclusively among the blacks, confers on the individual resistance to malaria. This might have been advantageous in the past for people living in an environment where malaria was prevalent. This example could very well be, and probably is, an exception. The point is, however, that we must not be too hasty in attempting to eliminate "defective" genes by eliminating people. To bring about an abortion is to eliminate from this life—and from the possibility of sharing the life Christ came to bring—a human person. No doubt a husband and wife do not want to bring a sick or malformed child into this life. It is possible in certain cases to predict that a particular couple will produce, say, a mongoloid child in one chance out of four. How badly do they want a child? Do they consider the difficulties such a child will meet in life? Yet it is one thing to decide not to conceive a child and it is another matter to abort the fetus once it is discovered that it has this particular disease. He already *is*. Can we act in his name and say that he would not wish to live? Furthermore, it is not clear in many cases to what extent a particular genetic condition will result in physical malformations and/or mental retardation.

Human anguish is difficult to measure. But sometimes pain is an occasion for growth. A person protected from all frustrations, sorrows, anxieties of life seems rather shallow and flabby of character. Is it too much to suggest that there may be an overconcern to create a Heaven on earth in lieu of what God through Christ promised us? Nonetheless, man is called to move forward: to conquer hunger, disease and ignorance, *in order* that he might enjoy a greater degree of creative and responsible freedom. But in our earnest strivings we need to recognize that there are limitations in what man can do to man, and what he can do to the earth. As sons of the Father we are each called to help bring about the eschatological community, the perfect fulfillment of God's dreams for man.

THE REFLECTION OF A PSYCHOLOGIST
MORRIS TAGGART, Ph.D.

The question before us in the Francoeur paper is this: Does the technological development in the area of human sexuality —all the way from oral contraceptives through extra-uterine pregnancy to the perfection of cloning—represent "revolutionary reality" that must be taken into account? If it does, what are the sources of value insight? Can social scientific analysis come up with anything close to what Donald Campbell of Northwestern calls "winnowed traditional wisdom?"

It is at this point that I find the partial answer of Francoeur very intriguing. He suggests that the presence of a true revolution may perhaps be detected in an area of human experience when the traditional language used to describe that area of human experience shows signs of serious strain. My own field of marital and family therapy is perhaps one such area of human experience. When a conflicted family is considered as the unit of intervention, the revolutionary nature of that way of understanding human hurt and pain may be detected in two ways. Within the psychic economy of the family itself, it is obvious that the traditional language of family intercourse is strained to the point where it may carry precious little meaning. There is the ubiquitous generation gap in which words convey very different meanings for the members of the family. Concepts of blame, causality and the like are no longer useful vehicles for meaning in family therapy. The cybernetic revolution has led to the attempt to understand the hurts of a family in a systemic framework and the concepts derived from the old "one-on-one" framework have limited usefulness at best.

Not only, however, is the family's language strained at this point. The new knowledge gained about family process has created difficulties for those professional disciplines involved with families. Just as families have discovered that the more traditional ways of understanding their interaction no longer suffice, so too have family therapists. Concepts that serve perfectly to illumine the diagnostic and treatment dimensions of an individual have either to be abandoned or radically modified when the unit of intervention is now a family. It is interesting to note that it is not only psychiatrists and other therapists who have had to cope with this new revolutionary reality. Legislators, judges and lawyers who have been involved in writing and practicing under the requirements of revised divorce laws have been very much in the same boat. The so-called "no fault" divorce laws that are operative in some states are indeed revolutionary when one remembers that the adversary system is deeply ingrained in American law.

It is interesting to note that the development of a systemic approach in family therapy is not just a matter of the therapist abandoning traditional psychiatric ways of thinking. In many cases the actual issues with which the conflicted family struggles are rather different also. Part of the task of the family therapist is to help the family articulate the value conflict rather than struggle with who is "crazy" and who isn't.

Another comment made by Dr. Francoeur would appear to be supported by clinical data drawn from conjoint family therapy. In discussing the patchwork quilt nature of a revolution in process, he made the remark that men may find it more difficult than women to deal with the implications of the sexual revolution. There are probably all sorts of reasons for this. Even from the biological standpoint, and I do not have the precise biological data at my finger tips, it would seem that the male of the species is more unstable around such things as sexuality, gender identification and the like than are females. It appears, for example, that whatever goes into gender identity, particularly from the hormonal side, is subject to very critical periods of development. If these critical periods of development are interfered with in some way, the chances are that something serious will appear later on in terms of gender identity. It may be important to note that among the 1,500 applications for sex reassignment surgery at the Gender Identification Unit at Johns Hopkins, there are twice as many men seeking sex reassignment as women.

We see things in family therapy that might point to the same kind of thing. Again, I am reporting data based more on clinical hunches than on systematic data collection, but the effect tends to be cumulative. First of all, there is the undoubted fact that women tend to initiate both marital and family therapy much more often than their husbands. Whatever the causes, it does seem that women do not regard the possible challenging of their marital and family operations in as threatening a light as do men. At our clinic we have begun to notice a kind of critical period in family therapy that revolves around the ability of the father to become vulnerable to the process. The critical period seems to occur fairly early on, say somewhere between the third and sixth session. The fathers are able to tolerate the process as long as they can sit on the sidelines, as it were. Often, the so-called "identified patient" is an adolescent and, while the focus is kept on this "crazy kid," father can enter into an alliance with the therapist, but as co-therapist rather than client. When the process begins to challenge father's operations within the psychic economy of the family and he is challenged to become part of the process, it would appear that more fathers than mothers simply cannot take it. Fathers, at least in our clinic sample, generally control the family finances in regard to things like therapy. It is at this critical period, therefore, that families tend to drop out of therapy. If father comes off the sidelines and becomes involved in the fray, the chances are that the family will persevere in the treatment.

It is clear that when we talk about sexuality we are talking about intimacy, and we are talking about the affective side of our lives. It is almost a truism to maintain that men have more difficulty in this area than do women, at least in the sense that men are taught to deal with it less openly. The American culture, with its northern European value system, provides many more options to women in dealing openly with affective material than it does men.

The fact that men are more vulnerable to the effects of the sexual revolution than are women is further complicated by the fact that it is men rather than women who tend to be the arbiters in matters of ethics and morality, at least when viewed overtly. It is men who tend to shape the ethical framework, even, in which the questions get discussed in the first place. Let me give you a striking example.

Someone was nasty enough to do an attitude survey of physicians on the question of whether or not they would offer sex reassignment surgery to those who asked for it. The survey instrument presented the clients under a number of conditions. One of the conditions was that the person asking for the surgery had had two years of psychotherapy and the psychiatrist had recommended that the surgery be done. Another condition was that the patient was seriously contemplating suicide if the surgery were not done. This last condition did not affect the distribution of the physicians' responses in the slightest. There were many doctors who apparently would rather that these patients be dead than that they would survive as persons who had their sex reassigned. I do not know the sex distribution of the doctors' survey but, if it were anything like the national average, the majority of them were men. Here again, most theologians, politicians and so on are men. Yet these, together with physicians and psychotherapists, are the groups of professionals who will make public policy relating to the sexual revolution. It is no longer evident to me that, as men and not women, they are in the best position to do so.

The final thing I would like to say is that if we do not know everything about all that is happening in the society, we do have the right and the responsibility to change what is happening in our own professional lives. It seems to me that, as we get more and more into issues like the sexual revolution, we have to think of some kind of confluence, some coming together of the disciplines. It seems clear that no more does there reside within one profession, and certainly not one professional, all of the answers to all of the questions in areas as complicated as this one. No one pretends that this is easy. We have tried it as much as anyone has here at the Institute of Religion and Human Development, and there are many struggles unresolved. Maybe the kind of model on which we might proceed is that proposed by Harvey Cox for the church when he challenged it to become a kind of "floating crap game." Maybe the model tends not to be very stable; it is somewhat opportunistic; it gets interested in this and then moves on to that. But perhaps, at this stage of the game, it provides the only means to bring the players in—the experts in ethics, medicine, psychology and all the rest. Then perhaps we can begin to winnow the traditional wisdom, whether that wisdom be expressed in ethical or scientific terms.

Again, I use a rather simple minded example. In our culture, it is quite acceptable for single women, whether divorced or widowed, to raise children. In fact, it is not only acceptable —it is considered desirable. This can be seen in data derived from decisions in child adoption proceedings and in child custody decisions and divorce actions. If psychologists were really involved in these processes, I think they might have raised serious questions about such practices long ago. Why? It is so acceptable in our culture for single women to raise children that it is quite likely that such a woman will end up as precisely that—a single woman who raises children. True, some women do remarry, or there may be times when a surrogate father enters the family, perhaps in the form of a minister, physician or family friend. If, however, we contrast this situation with what happens when a single man has to raise children, the situation is quite different. For one thing, he is more likely to marry after either divorce or the death of his spouse. Even if he does not remarry, people tend to break their necks to get surrogate mothers into that kind of situation. Maiden aunts come to live with them, the father hires a housekeeper and so on. What I am saying here is that, perhaps, from a psychological point of view and given our culture, children can better survive the loss of their biological mother than they can their biological father. Yet all the popular wisdom goes the other way.

I would like to see the kind of situation in which the psychologist could tug on the divorce judge's robe and say, "Hey! Have you thought of looking at the problem this way or that

way?" Similarly, the ethician might say to the medical re-
searcher, "How come this value which you have, and upon
which you proceed, has never really been allowed to see the
light of day?" Thus, each of us could challenge the other.

Such a "floating crap game" will not prevent the revolution,
whether sexual, racial, political or educational, nor is it designed to do so. For those of us who are not revolutionaries, it
may help to make the revolution more livable. For those of us
who are, it may help us get beyond the mere manning of the
barricades to the building of a new way of doing things.

POSTSCRIPT

j. edward carothers

The foregoing pages clearly demonstrate the urgent need for a new kind of life in the United States. Unless there is an immediate change in the ways we think and go about our business, bad matters will become worse. Some of our witless errors of the present could feed into troubles we will not be able to correct without painful and expensive wastes.

The United States has a basic responsibility to the whole world. In the United States the Christian churches hold a special responsibility for the ways of life practiced by the people of the nation. There are millions of adults and children related in some way to the various Christian churches. The opportunity for the churches in our time is greater than at any time in the past.

One of the troublesome barriers to getting the churches involved with the life-death issues raised in the preceding pages is the inability of many (if not most) church members to see any relationship whatsoever between what they think of as the Christian religion and all that is discussed here. How this blindness to the essential core of the Christian faith could have developed is a question to ponder.

At the heart of the Christian faith is the summons to a valid human life. This is defined in terms of love for neighbor and for God. In Christian faith God is not defined in a complicated metaphysic or theology. God is proclaimed as Father of all, Creator of all; the Harbor of destinies. The connection between these visions of God and the necessities posed by the issues raised in this book seems clear. It seems clear to some people, but not to Christians on a wide scale.

As Kenneth Vaux indicates in his introduction to this volume, the original impulse to hold the conference where the chapters of this book appeared as papers for discussion was started by participation in a meeting of the Task Force assigned by the National Council of Churches of Christ in the United States and Union Theological Seminary of New York to carry out a specific task. This assignment calls for a definition of "the necessary and possible agenda for the churches now."

The publication of the findings of the whole Task Force will take place November 1, 1972, and will also be published by Friendship Press. This suggests a connection between the two publications. It is a connection of mutual concern without any suggestion that a point of view is officially endorsed. Each point of view has to stand on its own merits; but when a point of view becomes an elevated spot from which one can see new ways toward a better life on this planet, it serves its highest function.

In a certain sense this volume is a good companion to the Task Force report, TO LOVE OR TO PERISH, which will be published later. It will also serve as an excellent resource for thoughtful discussion in the critical period that marks our lively decade.